The New Englishes

The New Englishes

John Platt
Heidi Weber
Ho Mian Lian

Routledge and Kegan Paul
London, Boston, Melbourne and Henley

First published in 1984
by Routledge & Kegan Paul plc

14 Leicester Square,
London WC2 7PH, England

9 Park Street, Boston, Mass. 02108, USA

464 St Kilda Road, Melbourne,
Victoria 3004, Australia and

Broadway House, Newtown Road,
Henley-on-Thames, Oxon RG9 1EN, England

Set in Press Roman 10 pt.
by Hope Services, Abingdon
and printed in Great Britain
by Billing & Sons Ltd, Worcester

Library of Congress Cataloging in Publication Data

Platt, John Talbot.

The new Englishes.
Bibliography: p.
Includes index.
1. English language – Foreign countries.   2. English
language – Study and teaching – Foreign speakers.
3. Bilingualism.   I. Weber, Heidi.   II. Lian, Ho Mian.
III. Title.
PE2751.P57   1984   427   83–26888

British Library CIP data available

ISBN 0-7100-9950-9
ISBN 0-7102-0194-X (pbk.)

Contents

Preface

When is a new English not a *New English*? When is something a learner's error and when is it part of a new language system? Are all New Englishes different because of differences in background languages and cultures or have they some things in common? Are there any problems if a New English is used as a standard for English teaching? Why do some creative writers use their New English and others not? All these and many more questions have intrigued us for some time and we have tried to tackle them in this book. Sometimes we may not have come up with a satisfactory answer, at least not for some readers. However we have tried to show the diversity, systematicity and, we hope, above all the legitimacy of some of the New Englishes.

We are indebted to numerous people as can be seen from our large bibliography. Many of them are authors from countries where the New Englishes are spoken. A special mention must be made of Braj Kachru and John Pride, who have done much to bring about an awareness of the existence of the New Englishes and to stimulate an interest in them.

Although much has been written on some New Englishes, little research has been done on others. In the area of Singapore and Malaysia, we have made use of data from our own research projects (1974-1983) some of which have been supported by ARGC and ARGS grants to J.T. Platt (ARGC Grants A68/16801 and A77/15355, ARGS Grant A280 15239). From some of the other areas, too, we have collected data, written and spoken.

However, our special thanks go to those many educated speakers of the different New Englishes who patiently answered our questions about their country, their English and language use in general. Without

vii

their generous help, we would have lost out on some interesting data.

And finally − thank you, June, for grappling so well with a manuscript full of crosses and arrows. We did appreciate it.

CHAPTER 1

New Englishes and New Nations

The spread of English to so many parts of the world and the increase in the number of those learning it and using it has been the most striking example of 'language expansion' this century if not in all recorded history. It has far exceeded that other famous case, the spread of Latin during the Roman Empire.

From being the language of a very small nation, England, the English language spread over the rest of the British Isles and from the early days of colonization in the Americas the pace increased. Some of this movement of English to other parts of the world has been by the migration of English-speaking people — to North America and later to Australia, New Zealand and South Africa. Speakers of English settled in new lands and continued to use English. It was also used in those colonies which were under British administration but where only a few British people settled permanently: places like India and Ceylon, West Africa, Malaya and islands in the Pacific, and in the West Indian colonies like Jamaica where small communities of English speakers dominated the West Africans who were brought there as slaves.

The end of the colonial era, however, has not seen a reversal of the spread of English. Many of the New Nations which were once British colonies have realized the importance of English not only as a language of commerce, science and technology but also as an international language of communication. In some of these nations, most of the education in schools and tertiary institutions is through the medium of English. Although other nations have decided to use an indigenous language as the medium of instruction in schools, English is nevertheless the main second language. With increased educational opportunities in these areas, more and more children are now either acquiring English as their first or at least as their second language.

The use of English has spread beyond those nations which were once part of the British Empire or were American possessions like the Philippines. English has become the most important international language and is the most commonly taught second or foreign language in the world. Strevens[1] gives a figure of over 600 million users of English of whom about half are native speakers and half have either picked up the language or have been taught it. Kachru[2] gives figures which add up to 115 million for enrolments in classes for formal English teaching throughout the world.

However, we are concerned here in particular with New Englishes. This means that we are interested not simply in speakers of English but in varieties of English. In particular, we are interested in new varieties of English. The term 'New Varieties' of English implies that there are more or less recognizable varieties spoken and/or written by groups of people. There are, of course, many *new speakers* of English all over the world but, as we shall discuss later in this chapter, they do not always speak a *New English*.

What, then, is a New English? As with any attempt at classification of languages or classification within a language, there is no precise, clear-cut answer. There are always borderline cases and cases which refuse to fit neatly into categories. However, we shall consider that a New English is one which fulfils the following criteria:

1 It has developed through the education system. This means that it has been taught as a subject and, in many cases, also used as a medium of instruction in regions where languages other than English were the main languages. The degree to which English is used as a medium of education for other subjects varies considerably from nation to nation and from one type of school to another.

2 It has developed in an area where a native variety of English was *not* the language spoken by most of the population. For various reasons, which we will discuss later, pidgin and creole languages are not considered to be *native varieties of English*.

3 It is used for a range of functions *among* those who speak or write it in the region where it is used. This means that the new variety is used for at least some purposes such as: in letter writing, in the writing of literature, in parliament, in communication between

the government and the people,|in the media and sometimes for spoken communication between friends and in the family. It may be used as a lingua franca, a general language of communication, among those speaking different native languages or, in some cases, even among those who speak the same native language but use English because it is felt to be more appropriate for certain purposes.

4 It has become 'localized' or 'nativized' by adopting some language features of its own, such as sounds, intonation patterns, sentence structures, words, expressions. Usually it has also developed some different rules for using language in communication.

Well-known examples of New Englishes include Indian English, Philippine English, Singapore English and African Englishes of nations such as Nigeria and Ghana. In all of these, English was introduced during the colonial era but was at first spoken and used mainly by native speakers of English from Britain and America. However, as there was a need for locally recruited clerks and other employees in government and business offices, schools were established in which English was taught and then used as the language of instruction for other subjects. Christian missions also played a part in the spread of English. Some missionaries did translate church services and parts of the Bible into local languages but many missions established schools where English was taught.

At first, the English-medium schools were staffed by teachers mainly from Britain or, in the case of the Philippines, from the USA. This does not mean, of course, that British teachers were always speakers of Standard Southern British English. In the early West African mission schools, for example, there were many missionaries/teachers from the north of England and Scotland and the influence of their speech on some features of West African English cannot be ruled out.[3]

With an increase in school enrolment and the establishment of more and more schools, it became necessary to recruit teachers who were not native speakers of English. In the beginning, they often came from areas where English had already established itself more firmly. This was the case in Singapore, Penang and Malacca where Indians, particularly Jaffna Tamils from Ceylon, were employed by the colonial administration as clerks and teachers.

However, teachers were also recruited locally. Some of those who had passed through the local schools were employed, and gradually teacher training colleges were established. Although these teachers attempted to use the formal English of the textbooks, their English differed considerably from that of the native speakers who had been their teachers. Brosnahan[4] sums up the situation for Southern Nigeria:

> The great majority of primary school teachers have themselves learnt English from other African teachers. . . . Primary school English . . . is thus a very interesting example of the teaching of a language being maintained at a fairly constant level by teachers who have relatively little contact with native speakers of that language.

In this way, children who were native speakers of various African and Asian languages acquired, in the school situation, a type of English that was already modified, that was different from the English of British or American native speakers. However, it was not only in the classroom that children learned English. They heard it from older children in the playground, on the way to school and on the way home. Many heard it at home from elder brothers and sisters. The English that these children acquired was good enough for talking to friends and it was particularly useful if those friends were native speakers of a language other than one's own. Even if some of the teachers called this 'broken English', it was, nevertheless, speech that served a purpose, the basic purpose of speech: that of communication with others.

As the education facilities increased, often with English as a medium of instruction, the number of speakers of English increased too. Not only was there an increase in the number of students enrolled but also in the range of education and the length of time that an individual student was able to attend school. Instead of only primary education, many students were gradually able to obtain secondary education and, particularly after the New Nations had gained their independence, students were able to enrol at local universities. This exposure to English from primary to secondary and, for some at least, to tertiary education contributed to an increase in the range and functions of the New Variety of English they were speaking. It was no longer only a colloquial variety used for communication with friends but it could be used for formal occasions and by educated speakers for all their everyday activities. Yet it had obtained a flavour of its own which could be recognized by its speakers as well as by outsiders.

We have talked about Indian English, Philippine English, Singapore

English, as if they were fixed entities with firmly established contours like, for instance, a marble statue or a particular type of motor car. Naturally, the matter is far more complex.

Jibril[5] raises the problem when he discusses *Nigerian English*. 'Nigerian English is defined as belonging to Nigeria but (quoting the Nigerian writer Achebe) still in communion with its ancestral home... altered to suit its new African surroundings.' And he goes on to say

> or is this English the *English language in Nigeria*? In this case, it
> is like an expatriate working on a short-term contract in Nigeria,
> housed in a secluded Government Reservation Area and generally
> not inclined to seek any social intercourse with local people. . . .

There are many ways in which one can try to define a specific New English.

One way would be a political approach, that is naming a variety after the nation where it is spoken, for example, *Nigerian English* for the English spoken in Nigeria. This may be a convenient quick way of solving the issue but it may overlook certain important factors. For example, with the new language policies in Malaysia which promote Malay as the national language, the language of government and of education, one should really talk of two kinds of *Malaysian English*. The 'old kind' is still spoken by English-medium educated older Malaysians and some younger Malaysian Chinese and Indians. This variety is very similar to Singapore English. The 'new' Malaysian English is spoken by the younger Malay-medium educated Malaysians.

Some people would favour narrower divisions. They would argue, for instance, that there is a considerable difference between Southern Nigerian English and Northern Nigerian English. Some would question the use of Caribbean English as there is quite a difference, at least in pronunciation, between varieties such as Jamaican English and Trinidadian English.[6] Naturally, the consideration of regional variation within a New English must not be neglected.

There is also the ethnic and/or language background of the speakers of the New Englishes. To what extent does Yoruba English differ from Hausa English in a Nigerian context? How far removed is the English of the non-Bantu speakers in Kenya from that of the Bantu speakers? Although there is an undoubted influence from the native languages of the speakers, we feel that there are, for example, common features shared by Panjabi English, Bengali English and Dravidian English which make them all recognizable as belonging to *Indian English*. In some cases, too, national-regional factors appear to obliterate ethnic and language background. This can be seen by the difference between the Indian English spoken by an Indian in India and the Singapore English spoken by an Indian in Singapore. Older Singapore Indians can often still be recognized as speakers of Indian English; younger Singaporeans of Indian background rarely can. Telephone tests conducted by the writers in Singapore showed that ethnically Chinese switchboard operators could identify English-medium educated younger Malays and Indians as 'Singaporeans' but could give no clue to their ethnicity.

We have already mentioned the importance of linguistic features such as sounds, sentence structures and special expressions which make it possible to define, even if only loosely, a particular New English. It is not possible to single out one feature, let us say a particular sound, because it may be shared by other New Englishes but, as Jibril[7] says when he discusses Nigerian English, 'If we can tell a Nigerian accent or text, we are usually able to do so because a number of co-occurrent features which *collectively* mark the accent or text as originating from Nigeria are all present.'

Looking at New Englishes in more general terms, one can see that they have many things in common. When we consider their present-day functions, they often have a high status in the nations where they are used as official or second language. Many of them are what Strevens[8] calls *Intra-Types*, that is they are used by groups within the country as a regular language for communication in at least some areas of everyday activity. We shall be talking more about the functions of the New Englishes in Chapter 2.

When looking at the background against which New Englishes developed, we can see that there are basically three different situations: (1) New Englishes developed in areas where education in English meant education in a language totally unlike the home languages of the pupils or the languages they would hear around them in the streets and markets. Before they came to school, children would have acquired a local language or, in multilingual nations, more than one local language. They might also have picked up a non-English language of communication, which could be used among people speaking different local languages, e.g. Bazaar Malay in Singapore and kiSwahili in Nairobi, Kenya. What we refer to as *local languages* could be languages which have been the native languages of the population for a long time, e.g. the various Indian languages in India, or it could mean languages which were spoken by immigrant groups which came to the area many decades or even a century ago. This would be the case in Singapore where in addition to Malay there are the southern Chinese dialects (Hokkien, Teochew, Cantonese, Hakka and Hainanese) and Indian languages such as Tamil, Panjabi and Bengali.

(2) In some parts of West Africa, especially along the coast of what are now Nigeria, Sierra Leone, Ghana, Gambia and parts of Cameroon, an English-based *pidgin* had developed. Various pidgins had been in use from the earliest days of European contact. Some had words mainly from English while others had their vocabulary mainly from Portuguese, Spanish, French or Dutch. All of them were simplified languages without such features as marking the verb for tenses, subject-verb agreement or differences between subject and object pronouns. A pidgin could be used not only for communicating with Europeans but also to serve as a language of communication, a lingua franca, among Africans speaking different languages.

Many children in these areas would therefore come to school already knowing an English-based pidgin. However, English-based pidgins are not native varieties of English. It is true that some of them are known at times as 'Pidgin English' because much of their vocabulary is derived from English. But many words are so changed in pronunciation and meaning that learning English really meant learning an almost totally new range of words. In addition, the grammar of English and the grammar of the pidgin are completely different.[9] English-based pidgins cannot be considered as New Englishes as they do not fulfil our first criterion. They have not developed through the education system. They were not taught but developed to perform the basic needs of communication among people who would otherwise have had no language in common. This does not mean that Pidgin in West Africa is not an extremely important language of communication. In fact, from all accounts its use as a lingua franca is increasing, particularly in the more informal areas of everyday activity.

(3) In some parts of the world, English has been taught in schools to speakers of an English-based *creole*. A creole is a speech variety which has developed from a pidgin. This is normally the case when a pidgin fulfils more and more of the functions of a native language for a group of speakers, being used for much or most of the communication in everyday life. As a very basic pidgin is inadequate for normal everyday use, for talking about all the things people want to talk about, the pidgin is expanded in various ways. New words are added and a more complex grammatical system develops. In this way, English-based creoles

7

developed in the former British possessions in the Caribbean, such as Jamaica, Trinidad and the former British Guiana (now Guyana).

As education through the medium of English became available, a situation developed with people speaking a whole range of speech varieties from the creole to a type close to Standard English. Such a situation has become known as a *post-creole speech continuum.*[10] Those with little or no formal education speak the creole or a slightly modified creole. We shall refer to this as the *basilect*. The type of speech closest to Standard English is the *acrolect*. This would be spoken, at least in more formal situations, by those with higher levels of education. The types of speech between the basilect and the acrolect are referred to as *mesolects*. A post-creole continuum is represented in Figure 1.

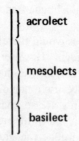

acrolect

mesolects

basilect

Figure 1 Post-creole continuum

The acrolect and some of the mesolects of a post-creole continuum can certainly be considered as New Englishes. We can speak of a Jamaican English, Trinidadian English, Guyanian English and so on, or a Caribbean English in general. There are differences in pronunciation and in vocabulary and to some extent in grammatical structure between these Englishes and the kinds of English spoken in Britain but at the 'upper' end of the continuum they can certainly be considered as varieties of English. The problem is, however, that there is no clear point along the continuum where it can be said 'This is no longer English.'

The creoles themselves or speech close to them at the basilectal end of the speech continuum cannot be considered as New Englishes. They did not develop through the education system but from pidgins. They are, in themselves, interesting speech varieties. Because they are used by their speakers for a range of everyday functions, they have a larger vocabulary and more complex sentence structure than the typical pidgins. However, although the English-based creoles contain English words, the meanings of these words often differ considerably from related words in English and the word forms and sentence structures of these creoles cannot be considered as part of the grammar of English. Although an English-based creole is a native language variety because it has speakers who use it as their first, and often their only, language, it cannot be considered as a native variety of *English*. [11]

If we divide the New Englishes according to the background against which they developed, we can distinguish three different types:

Type	Background	Examples
1	local language(s) usually non-English language of wider communication	Indian English Kenyan English Singapore English
2	local language(s) English-based pidgin used as language of wider communication (in some areas)	Ghanaian English Nigerian English
3	English-based creoles	Caribbean English

Naturally, there are cases which do not fit neatly into either category. One example is English in Papua New Guinea. In some parts, especially in the towns, the local English-based pidgin, Tok Pisin, has been modified because of English-medium films, radio broadcasts and English language newspapers and magazines. There has also been a gradual shift in the functions of Tok Pisin. Although it is still a pidgin for some, that is a language of communication between people of different language groups, it has become a native language for others. For them, it can be considered a creole.

It may be asked whether there are some other types of New Englishes which we have so far overlooked. In order to answer this question, we shall look briefly at four types of English which may in some ways seem to be 'newer Englishes' but which we do not include under the *New Englishes* for reasons given below.

1 Native varieties other than British English

American English, Australian English, New Zealand English, Canadian

English and South African English are all in a sense *new* Englishes. They developed differently from the way English developed in Britain. People from various parts of Britain were mixed together in the new settlements and colonies and there was a mixture of many accents and dialects. In addition, there has been considerable immigration to these areas by speakers of many other languages. The USA has been referred to as the 'melting pot' and Australia, too, has experienced similar mass immigration in the last thirty years.

However, all the varieties of English mentioned above differ from the New Englishes because there has been a continuity in the use of English. People came to these areas speaking English and remained speaking English. Other immigrant groups were absorbed into the main body of English speakers. It has been different with the New Englishes. English was, in most cases, at first a language learned at school. This is still usually the case, although there are now in various new nations minorities for whom a New English is a native language.

2 The Newer Englishes of the British Isles

English has, of course, a shorter history in some parts of the British Isles than in others. In Ireland, Wales, parts of Scotland and even in the southwestern English county of Cornwall, English is a comparatively new language. It is well known that for many years the Welsh language was suppressed and education available only in English. However, the influence of Welsh persisted in the pronunciation, including intonation, and in some grammatical structures of Welsh English. The same is true of Ireland and parts of Scotland where Gaelic was spoken and is still used to some extent. We shall not, however, consider these as types of New English. In some of these areas the movement to English occurred before education was generally available and furthermore this change has taken place in areas relatively close to a large population of native speakers of English.

3 Immigrant English

It could be argued that the types of English spoken by immigrants who spoke a language other than English and who came to English-speaking nations such as Britain, the USA and Australia are also New Englishes.

Certainly, the types of English spoken by these immigrants are new. In some cases they may be recognizable as distinctive types such as Italian-influenced, Greek-influenced or Turkish-influenced. However, they occur in areas where a native variety of English is spoken by most of the population, whereas the New Englishes have developed in areas where a native variety of English was *not* the main language (our second criterion).

In many cases, immigrant Englishes are temporary phenomena. For example, in Australia, although immigrants may speak with a noticeable foreign accent and use sentence structures which would not be used by native speakers, their children will probably speak the type of Australian English of their peer group. At most, they may display very slight traces of a foreign accent. By the next generation there is typically no recognizable difference from the speech of Anglo-Australians.

4 'Foreign' English

The last type of English which might be considered is the type of English spoken by those who have acquired it as a foreign language. It is true that we speak, for instance, of English with an Italian, German or Swedish accent but hardly of Italian, German or Swedish English as a language variety in its own right. Although English may be used for communicating with English-speaking foreigners, for reading, for listening to English language radio broadcasts and watching English language films, English in countries such as Italy, Germany and Sweden does not fulfil our third criterion for a New English. It is not typically used for purposes of communication within these countries.

The New Englishes, as we have seen, have developed through English-medium education either in areas where English-based pidgins or creoles were spoken or where local languages and possibly a non-English lingua franca were used by the majority of the people. The type and the range of functions of these New Englishes vary considerably from nation to nation.

In the next chapter we shall look more closely at the functions of the New Englishes in various parts of the world. In later chapters we shall see the ways in which some of the New Englishes, although spoken in widely separated parts of the world, are strikingly similar. However, we shall also see that in other ways there are great differences. Just as it is usually possible to distinguish Americans from Australians or

New Zealanders by the way they speak English, it is usually possible to distinguish West Africans from Indians or Singaporeans. Unfortunately, many of the New Englishes have not yet been adequately studied and described. Because of this, our discussion of some features of New Englishes will necessarily be restricted to those where a reasonable amount of investigation has been undertaken or where we were able to collect our own data. Overall, however, we hope to show the diversity and the unity, the richness and the creativeness of the New Englishes.

CHAPTER 2

The role of English

There are many factors which will determine whether a particular language or a variety of language will develop or dwindle away. If it develops – it matters also how it develops. Is there, for instance, only a formal style or is there a whole range of styles, including a robust dynamic colloquial one? Much of this development or regression depends on where and when a language is used and by whom, what the attitudes of the people in the community are to the language and, a very important factor, what the government attitude is to it. Does a government merely recognize that a language is used, does it discourage its use or does it promote its use? Promoting a language can be done in many ways. One is to make it the national language or one of the official languages. Another way is to make it the medium of education or one of the media of education.

In nations such as Britain, the USA, Australia and New Zealand, English would be the *national* language as well as the *official* language, although this may not always be overtly stated. The difference between national and official language is usually of no significance in these countries. In New Nations, this is different. The term national language is one that has connotations of belonging to a nation, of ethnic and/or cultural identity. A national language is usually a local language spoken as native language by at least some of the population of a nation, for example Malay (Bahasa Malaysia) in Malaysia and kiSwahili in Kenya and Tanzania. An official language is generally used for government administration and the Higher Courts of Law, in the media and as one of the languages of education, at least of secondary and higher education.

The choice of English as an official language in many of the New

Nations is not surprising. The reason is not only that English had been the language of the former colonial administration and was therefore the popular choice for an elite group. English has also become, the world over, a language for international communication, diplomacy and business dealings. It has been one of the major languages used for scientific and technological research and publications.

A further point is that in multilingual nations it can be considered a neutral language of communication. Moag[1] when discussing the position of English in Fiji, remarks that 'this neutrality is political in character, i.e. giving no group the advantage of having its own language singled out for official status' and Akere[2] says about English in Nigeria, 'The multi-ethnic situation in Nigeria and the accompanying emotional attachment to ethnic identity by various groups required the adoption of a neutral language.'

Table 1 lists the main nations and territories in which English had or still has official or semi-official status and where New Englishes have developed or are developing. Except for the countries which are marked with an asterisk, English is also one of the main media of education.

A language, particularly in bilingual and multilingual nations, must be looked at against the background of the other languages of the region with which it shares its functions in the community. This is also relevant for the New Englishes. English may have been or still be the national language, the official language or one of the official or semi-official languages in a New Nation. However, where language is concerned, nothing is static. In some nations, English is spreading at the expense of the local languages. In other nations, a local language has become the national language and taken over the place that was once occupied by English. In others again, English has been replaced as national and even as the main official language but because of increased educational opportunities more children than ever are acquiring it as their second language and its status is again increasing. One could say that it is 'coming in by the back door'.

A brief discussion of the language situation in some of the main nations mentioned in our table may give a clearer picture of the overall position of English.

A common factor which is shared by the nations in East and West Africa is the enormous number of separate indigenous languages. Writers vary about the estimated number of languages spoken in any one nation but numbers between 80 and 400 have been quoted,[3] depending on the size and ethnic diversity of a nation. Some, of course, are mutually intelligible — others are not.

Table 1

AFRICA

    West Africa   *East Africa*
    Cameroon   Kenya
    Gambia   Tanzania*
    Ghana   Uganda
    Liberia   Zambia
    Nigeria   Zimbabwe
    Sierra Leone

AMERICA   ASIA

    Caribbean Region   Bangladesh*
    Barbados   Hong Kong
    Belize   India*
    Guyana   Malaysia*
    The Leeward Islands   Pakistan*
    Jamaica   Philippines*
    Puerto Rico   Singapore
    Trinidad and Tobago   Sri Lanka*
    The Windward Islands

PACIFIC

    Cook Islands
    Fiji
    Guam
    Hawaii
    Papua New Guinea
    Samoa (Western Samoa and American Samoa)
    Solomon Islands

However, one way in which West African and East African nations differ, linguistically speaking, is that in West Africa English-based pidgins and creoles have developed whereas there was no such development in East Africa. Varieties of an English-based pidgin, which first started in the West African ports to serve as a means of communication between sailors and traders and the local population, spread along the coastal areas from Gambia to Cameroon.

The use of Pidgin English as a language of communication has been increasing steadily. Shnukal[4] writes about Nigerian Pidgin English that

> in spite of penalties for using it in school and in spite of its
> reputation as a language for 'illiterates', its lack of standardized
> spelling and its consequent lack of prestige and official recognition,

NPE is continuing to gain speakers. . . . It is now the lingua franca of two southern states, Bendel and Rivers, and of large southern cities such as Lagos.

The language of the freed American slaves who were settled in Sierra Leone, particularly in and around the capital Freetown, was an English-based creole, called Krio. As Krio speakers were in demand as missionaries, clerks and teachers in various areas of West Africa, their speech had a marked influence on many varieties of West African English.[5]

However, the influence of Pidgin English on West African Englishes is also considerable. When children in southern coastal towns start their formal education in English, many are already speakers of Pidgin English. In spite of government discouragement, many primary teachers use Pidgin English, at least in the early stages of primary education.[6] In the words of a primary school teacher in Cameroon: 'For the first six months I have to use Pidgin. If I didn't, the children would not understand *one word*. Only after I have trained them in Pidgin can I begin to use proper English.'[7]

Apart from the United Republic of Cameroon where English shares its position as official language with French, it obviously has high official status in Sierra Leone, Gambia, Ghana and Nigeria. However, one should not underestimate the importance of the major indigenous languages in the area, e.g. Akan, Ewe, Ga and Hausa in Ghana and Hausa, Igbo and Yoruba in Nigeria. Their influence extends over a wide area. For instance, Hausa, the main language of Northern Nigeria, is used in various parts of West Africa as a language of wider communication and has on occasion been proposed as a candidate for a national language of Nigeria.[8] Although English is the medium of instruction in secondary and tertiary education, the major indigenous languages are encouraged as school subjects, if not as compulsory then as optional subjects. For example, in Ghana the major languages Akan, Ga, Ewe and Hausa are examination subjects and to take one of them is compulsory for the first three years of secondary schooling. In Nigeria, it is the National Policy of Education that 'each Nigerian child should be encouraged to learn one of the three major languages [that is Hausa, Igbo or Yoruba] other than his mother tongue. . .'.[9]

Primary education may be officially in English or, as in Nigeria[10] the first three years in the main local languages. In reality, the language of instruction often depends on the region − north or south, urban or rural − the school and the availability of teachers.

The overall situation of English in the West African nations we discussed above can be seen in Table 2.

Table 2

	Official medium of instruction (incl. lang. of textbooks)	*Unofficial medium of instruction*	*Position of local languages*
Primary	English or major local languages	Krio, Pidgin or local languages	compulsory or encouraged
Secondary	English	English	compulsory or encouraged
Tertiary	English	English	encouraged

It must be mentioned that for Cameroon this is valid only for the part which was formerly under British administration. The role of English is taken by French in the rest of the nation.

In parts of East Africa, the major language of wider communication has not been an English-based pidgin, as in the West, but kiSwahili, a Bantu language. KiSwahili is the native language of relatively few speakers, mainly along the coast and in Zanzibar (now part of Tanzania). It was used by Arab traders from Zanzibar on inland trading routes for slaves and ivory and spread rapidly over other areas of East Africa. In Tanzania it has become the national language and has replaced English as a medium of instruction in schools. It is the national language of Uganda and of Kenya but English is still an official language there and enjoys a high social status. In Zambia, English is the official language and the medium of instruction at schools. Zimbabwe (formerly Rhodesia) is somewhat different from the rest as it had a larger group of native speakers of English who formed an elite.

However, as in West Africa, the major local languages of the East African nations must not be ignored. For example, in Zambia where 80 different local languages and/or dialects are spoken, Bemba, Lozi, Nyanja and Tonga are of particular importance. They are among the seven language varieties which have been given official recognition as languages of the state, are 'used for written and oral government propaganda'[11] and are also taught at school. They are used as languages of wider communication in their particular region with Nyanja functioning as a lingua franca in the capital Lusaka. As an educated Zambian puts it: 'Although official language is English, there are some cases where you need to know one of the national languages. People usually know one of them. They don't want to show that they come from a smaller tribe.'

As far as education is concerned, the situation in most of these African nations is similar to that in West Africa, except that kiSwahili is playing a double role. In a pidgin form it has the role which Pidgin English and Krio have in West Africa and in an educated form it has taken over from English in at least one of the nations.

The difference between the various East African nations we have mentioned can be seen in Table 3.

Table 3

| | Medium of education | | | Main second languages |
	Primary	*Secondary*	*Tertiary*	
Kenya	urban: English rural: (first years) kiSwahili or regional language	English	English	kiSwahili (usually from Primary 4)
Uganda	(first years) local languages or kiSwahili (later years) English	English	English	kiSwahili
Zambia	(first years) major local languages (later years) English	English	English	A major local language
Tanzania	(local languages) kiSwahili	Forms 1–4: kiSwahili Forms 5–6 still English	English	From Primary 4 English

The situation in Tanzania is an interesting one. Matters are still in transition but, no doubt, the complete change-over from English to kiSwahili in the school system will have an effect on Tanzanian English. As one English-medium educated Tanzanian put it: 'If you complete Form 6 and go to university here or abroad, those people require

English, but kids in secondary schools will be less conversant with English as we were in our times.'

The English in all the Caribbean countries and territories which we mentioned in Table 1 belongs to our type 3 as far as its background is concerned. This means that in the areas where English is the official language and language of education, the main local language is an English-based creole – or rather, different varieties of creole. They developed from English-based pidgins spoken by West-African slaves who were brought to the area as plantation workers. In some areas, e.g. Jamaica and Belize, some Spanish is spoken and on some of the islands there are also a few Asian languages, e.g. Hakka, a Southern Chinese dialect, in Jamaica and Hindi in Trinidad and Tobago.[12] However, these are negligible when compared to Creole. Most children coming to school to learn English were already speakers of Creole. Early instruction in school, particularly informal explanation by the teacher, was in Creole. Its use in informal situations is widespread, even among educated speakers of Caribbean English. Like the local languages, and to some extent the pidgins and Krio in Africa, it signifies for its speakers a feeling of belonging, of shared local beliefs and images and its influence on Caribbean English is marked, particularly as far as pronunciation is concerned.

In Asia the situation is far more complex. Six of the nations mentioned in Table 1, all former British or American colonies or protectorates, have since chosen a language other than English as their national language and main medium of instruction, namely:

Bangladesh	Bengali
India	Hindi (a language spoken natively in northern India)
Malaysia	Bahasa Malaysia (Malay)
Pakistan	Urdu
Philippines	Pilipino (Tagalog)
Sri Lanka	Sinhala

However, English still plays an extremely important part in these nations.

In India, a great number of different local languages are spoken. Although Hindi is now the official language of the Union of India, English is the 'associate official language' and the sole official language in several states and territories.[13] It is also one of the important languages used in the press, for literature and still used extensively in

19

government offices. For example Mehrotra[14] states that out of 2,662 telegrams issued by the Ministry of Education to the state governments and subordinate offices during a three-month period in 1975 only 20 were in Hindi, 2,642 were in English. English is available as a medium of instruction in several Indian states. Parasher[15] talks about the great public demand for English-medium education in recent years:

> There is always a great rush for admission to English-medium schools. . . . Although both Hindi and English are available as media of instruction in the government-run Central Schools and Sainik Schools, a large majority of children admitted to these schools opt for English.

In Sri Lanka, the main local languages are Sinhala and Tamil. In parts of the country there are large groups of Tamil speakers, descendants of former immigrants from Southern India. English was replaced as the language of administration as early as 1956 by Sinhala, with some use of Tamil. Later on, Sinhala also took over from English as the major medium of education for primary, secondary and most of tertiary education.[16] Education at all levels is also available in Tamil. There are some prestigious government schools and some private colleges which have instruction available in either Sinhala, Tamil or English: otherwise English is taught as a subject. According to an educated Singhalese:

> I think English is deteriorating. . . . English is essential subject up to Grade 10 [GCE Ordinary Level] but English is not taught that effectively in the countryside, you know, even as subject. There is rush to city schools because parents are eager to give children some knowledge of English language. So there's a big influx of students from country to city.

At present, English is still an important language, particularly in larger urban centres and as a language of wider communication between educated Singhalese and Tamils.

In the Philippines, a group of about 7,000 islands where more than 70 different local languages and dialects are spoken, the main local languages are Tagalog, Cebuana, Ilocano, Hiligaynon, Biko and Waray.[17] As the Philippines were administered by the USA, English had been the main language of administration and education. It is still an important official language but, after independence, pressure for an indigenous national language resulted in the adoption of a modified version of Tagalog, known as Pilipino. Andrew Gonzalez[18] summed up the situation when he commented:

> Short of massive social upheaval or a radical change in the politics
> of the region, the Filipino will continue to be multilingual, at least,
> trilingual, using the local vernacular as the language of the home,
> Tagalog-based Pilipino as an urban lingua franca, and English as
> the language of commerce, legislation, government and international
> relations, perhaps using Pilipino and English as the language of
> education. . . .

In primary and secondary education, however, English is only the
language of instruction for science and mathematics. Fishman[19] calls
them 'ethnically less encumbered subjects'. The rest of the primary
and secondary education is in Pilipino. Fishman states that 'this policy
is in line with the. . . re-ethnification goals of the local authorities, who
recognize, at the same time, that English reigns supreme in the econo-
technical area.' He goes on to say that in the Philippines ' "a little bit of
English for almost everyone" is considered a good thing as is a lot of
English for a select few, provided the language can be confined to its
allotted domain.'

A similar attitude appears to have been prevailing among some of
the educated Malays in Malaysia. 'You don't need English in Malaysia
to buy postage stamps and the like,' was the statement of a prominent
Malaysian to one of the writers, 'in fact all that is needed for the bulk
of the population is a reading knowledge of the language. Only a select
group of educated Malaysians need to know English fluently, as they
have to make the contact with the outside world.' Now the pendulum
is swinging again and the 'falling standard of English' is bemoaned by
government authorities and measures have been suggested to 'stop
the decline'.

The movement to Bahasa Malaysia (a somewhat modified and
formalized Malay) as the national language and the medium of instruction in schools and at tertiary institutions is fairly recent. The
conversion process in schools took place between 1970 and 1982. Until
the late 1960s, English had been an extremely important language in
government, administration and in education. The enrolment in English-
medium secondary schools in 1967 was as high as 69.1 per cent.[20]
Malay is by no means the only language in the region. In addition to
Aboriginal languages there are the southern Chinese dialects, particularly Hokkien and Cantonese, spoken by the descendants of Chinese
immigrants, who form about 40 per cent of the total population. There

is also Tamil, the most widely used Indian language in Malaysia and other Indian languages.

By the late 1960s an interesting New English had developed in Malaysia. It was spoken as second language by many — as a first language by some Eurasians, Chinese and Christian Indians. We have already mentioned that it was very similar to that spoken in Singapore. Since then, the Malaysian English of the younger generation has changed from a true second language to something bordering on a foreign language.

Any language can be considered as a *foreign language*, a *second language* or a *native language*, depending on a number of factors such as the competence that the speakers have in the language, the functions it fulfils in a community and at what stage the speakers may have acquired the language. The term second language may be used in two ways. In the USA it may cover the whole range of non-native languages. We are using it here in the way commonly used in Britain and distinguish it from the concept of foreign language.

Important factors which determine whether a language can be classed as a foreign, second or native language are the type and the range of functions which a language has in a community. Often, of course, there is no clear-cut division and many varieties can be considered as being more or less foreign, second or native languages. For some speakers in a New Nation, English may be a native or near native language, whereas for others it is still a second language. Increase or decrease in the everyday use of the language may affect the structure of a language as a whole, e.g. its sound system, its sentence structures, its vocabulary and even its range of styles. As can be seen from Figure 2, a New English which may have been a second language in a country may expand its functions and gradually become more and more a native or near-native language for many of its speakers. This is the case with English in Singapore. However, in a country where the use of English is decreasing and where it serves fewer and fewer functions, it may gradually become a foreign language. This may be the case with English in Malaysia in the future.[21]

The language situation in Singapore is probably unique. It has been described in detail in Platt and Weber *English in Singapore and Malaysia*. Here we shall give only a brief sketch. About 76 per cent of the Singapore population are Chinese, descendants of immigrants from southern China, 15 per cent are Malay and about 7 per cent Indians, mainly Dravidians. The main Chinese dialect spoken is Hokkien; others

EFL	ESL	ENL

←· — — — — — — — — — — — — — →
decrease in functions   increase in functions

EFL = English as a foreign language
ESL = English as a second language
ENL = English as a native language

Figure 2

are Teochew, Cantonese, Hakka and Hainanese. In addition to its use by the 42 per cent of Chinese who are Hokkien, the Hokkien dialect is also used as a wider language of communication by speakers of different Chinese dialects. The four official languages of Singapore are English, Mandarin, Malay and Tamil. Although Mandarin has only about 1 per cent of native speakers in the area, it is considered by the government as a more suitable language than any of the southern Chinese dialects for the expression of Chinese values and culture. There have been several campaigns urging the Chinese population of Singapore to speak 'more Mandarin and less dialect'.

English is growing steadily in status, functions and as the major language of education. In principle, any of the four official languages can be chosen as a medium of instruction, with English as a second language if it is not chosen as the first language. If English is chosen as the medium of instruction, then either Mandarin, Malay or Tamil must be taken as a compulsory second language. In reality, Tamil-medium education has vanished. Malay-medium education is dwindling. Many of the Chinese-medium schools have changed over to an essentially English-medium education, teaching Chinese only as a subject. Lately, there have been moves to provide monolingual education, mainly in English or Chinese, for the less gifted children and to encourage students with more academic ability to go to special bilingual schools. There the aim is for them to become proficient in English *and* Chinese. All tertiary education in Singapore is in English.

As many younger Singaporeans take Mandarin or Malay as their compulsory second language at school, they are in fact at least bi-lingual and, if they are Chinese, usually tri- or quadri-lingual. For most of the younger generation, English has taken over from Bazaar Malay, a pidgin-type Malay, as the language of communication between ethnic groups. It is the language of administration, of the law courts and most of commerce. It is the language that promises more status, advance-ment and better-paid jobs.

Unlike Singapore which has an ethnically mixed population, 98 per cent of the population of the British colony of Hong Kong are Chinese. Most of them originated from Guangdong, a southern Chinese province, and are speakers of Cantonese. Other dialects of Chinese are spoken by minority groups but Cantonese is the lingua franca in Hong Kong. Although a number of Hong Kong Chinese are able to speak Mandarin (Putonghua), it is not generally used as a language of wider communication and it has no official status.[22] The two official languages in Hong Kong are English and Cantonese.

English is still the main language used in dealings between the government and the people and for most proceedings in the law courts. English is also one of the media of instruction in schools and universities. Primary education is mainly in Cantonese. There are two types of secondary schools, the 'Anglo-Chinese Schools' where English is the official medium of instruction and the 'Chinese Middle Schools' where Cantonese is the medium of instruction and English only a subject. University education is available in Chinese (at the Chinese University) or in English (at the University of Hong Kong).

Luke and Richards,[22] when discussing the language situation in Hong Kong, state that English 'is neither a foreign language nor a second language' and we think they are right as far as the statement refers to the overall situation. At present English holds a very strange position in Hong Kong. It is an official language and the native language of a small elite group of 'outsiders'. It is a second language for an elite group of bilingual local Chinese who speak it with fluency but rarely among themselves. It is used by many Chinese professionals, clerks and secretaries mainly as a written language, although some oral proficiency in English is often desired by larger employers.[23] However, the majority of the lower-middle-class and working-class population of Hong Kong know little or no English.

And yet, demand for English-medium education is growing steadily. According to Luke and Richards:[22]

> In 1979 the number of E.-m. [English-medium] schools in Hong Kong totalled about 80% of all secondary schools in Hong Kong and the number of students in these schools amounted to almost 90% of the entire secondary school population. . . . These figures reflect a gradual shift in parental attitudes towards English education, since success in the E.-m. system is seen to lead to better employment prospects for the children.

The two countries in the Pacific where English is an important official language are Fiji and Papua New Guinea. About half of the people of Fiji are Indians, mainly speakers of Hindi, who are descendants of immigrant labourers and merchants, and about 45 per cent are Fijians. Their language, Fijian, is an Austronesian language. English is the main language of government, commerce and education. In the first three years of primary education, children are taught in the local languages, with English as a subject. After that, English is the medium of instruction[24] but Fijian or Hindi may be taken as second language. English has also become an important wider language of communication between the various ethnic groups. Moag and Moag[25] comment:

> In Fiji, Chinese, Fijians, Indians and Rotumans all speak their own
> language at home or even when chatting with each other in public,
> but in situations of both formal and informal contact across
> communal lines – Church services, meetings, grog sessions, games,
> etc. – an appropriate variety of English is generally used.

Papua New Guinea has over 700 local languages. Two languages of wider communication have developed: Police Motu, now called Hiri Motu, in the south of the country, and an English-based pidgin, Tok Pisin, in the northern parts. Tok Pisin has developed in structure and vocabulary and has expanded its functions and its influence over a large area of the country. Taylor[26] states that Tok Pisin is now spoken by half or more of the population of Papua New Guinea.

English is the official language of administration and much government business is carried on in English. English is officially the sole medium of education from primary to tertiary, although there have been moves lately to allow the use of local languages in the first two years of primary school.[26] Although English is used in formal situations, the main language for wider communication in informal situations is undoubtedly Tok Pisin. As an educated New Guinean put it:

> Pidgin is becoming the second national language for people to
> communicate with. . . . Like in the offices or where people work,
> people use English but when they come out of offices and they are
> on the street – on the street, if I meet someone from another
> province, we speak in Pidgin – not English.

When we look at the overall use of English in new nations, we can find certain patterns of use. Except for nations like Malaysia, Sri Lanka and Tanzania which have opted for a local language as national language, areas where English is predominant are government administration and the higher courts of law. In the proceedings of lower courts, local languages and the local lingua franca are often used together with English. Usually, however, written records are kept in English. English is used by professionals, e.g. doctors, lawyers, dentists, at least among themselves and to their educated clients. In many nations, such as India, it is used by university and college staff, in conferences and discussions and often in lectures and tutorials. It is the language of most business correspondence and, particularly in larger firms, it is also the language of upper-level employees.

Except in places where there is a local film industry, such as the Philippines[27] and India, which support films in the national languages, many films shown are in English – particularly in the urban areas. However, where local languages are also spoken outside the nation, countries sometimes import films in these languages, e.g. Singapore imports films in Chinese (formerly in Cantonese, now predominantly in Mandarin).

In radio and television, English often shares broadcast time with other official languages. For example, in Zambia,

General Service: approx. 90% in English
                            10% in the major local languages
Home Service: uses no English but mainly four of
                        the major local languages

In addition to importing books in English, several new nations, e.g. India, Singapore and Nigeria, have a vigorous group of local writers producing works in English. We shall discuss the use of the New Englishes in literature in a later chapter.

In some nations, e.g. Ghana and Zambia, most of the daily papers are published in English. In others, English language newspapers are important and have a wide distribution. In India, for example, English language newspapers are published in 27 of the 29 Indian states and union territories and their total circulation is the highest of any of the different language newspapers in India.[28] Even in nations where English is no longer the national/official language, there are still important English-language dailies such as the *New Straits Times/New Sunday Times* in Malaysia.

In more informal areas of everyday communication, English often plays a less important role in some of the nations. In countries where the official language of education is English, pidgins, creoles or local languages may also be used in the playground or for more informal discussion between students and teachers in class. As we have mentioned already, even if English is the official language at work, pidgins, creoles or local languages may be used when talking to colleagues and friends. In countries such as Singapore, however, where the local English has a wider range than in some other nations, speakers may use a more colloquial form of Singapore English when speaking to friends. Among educated people in some multilingual nations, English is often one of the languages used when their friends are of different language backgrounds from their own. In other nations it may also be used even among friends of the same language background, e.g. English-educated Hokkien Chinese in Singapore.

In a number of the New Nations, there are small groups of native speakers of the New English who would use English exclusively in the home. Usually, however, the home is the last territory to give way to English. Most of the educated Africans we interviewed stated that they would still use their local language in the home, particularly with their parents and older relatives. With the increase in English-medium education, it is likely that the use of English in the home will increase. Platt and Weber[29] compared the use of English by Singaporeans who had had an English-medium education with those who had not. As can be seen in Table 4, there is a considerable difference between the two groups.

Table 4

| | Speakers who use English (%) to | | | | |
	Father	Mother	Husband/ wife	Brothers/ sisters	Children
English-medium educated	36	12	61	71	100
Non-English-medium educated	0	0	36	34	75

We have already seen that two aspects are of importance when we are talking about the role of English in New Nations. One is whether we refer to the written or spoken use of English and the other one is the use of English in relation to the type and level of education of the speakers. In most of the new nations, high levels of English-medium education also mean higher paid jobs and higher social status. In some nations, such as Singapore, Nigeria and Ghana, the New Englishes have developed a noticeable range of different varieties linked strongly to the socio-economic and educational backgrounds of their speakers.

There is a third aspect which must be considered when talking about the role of English. This is the regional aspect. Not only may there be variations in the actual variety of English between different regions of a country but there are usually also differences in the extent to which English is used. In some nations there is a considerable difference in the use of English between, for instance, the northern parts and the southern parts, between the coastal regions and inland and particularly between the urban centres and the rural areas. For example, there is more overall use of English in Lagos and other urban centres of Nigeria and in the southeastern part than in the rest of the country. In Malaysia, there has always been more use of English in Penang and Malacca, two of the former British Straits Settlements, and in Kuala Lumpur, the capital, than there has been in the northeastern predominantly Malay states of Kelantan and Trengganu. Sometimes, there is even a difference between various districts or suburbs of urban centres. These regional or area differences are particularly noticeable when we talk about what language is used for transactions, such as shopping. In most of the new nations English is often used in large department stores and expensive shops in city areas. In small shops in outer suburban and particularly in rural areas a non-English lingua franca or one of the local languages would most commonly be used. For example, an educated Zambian commented:

> In high-class shops in urban area, you use English − even to a fellow African. You cannot know which tribe he belongs. But different in rural areas. You often use local languages.

And from an educated Kenyan:

> In small shops most of the time you use Swahili − sometimes local languages. In high-class shops you use English. If you go into high-class shop, they think you have money. Having money in Kenya means you also speak English.

English in the New Nations has two important types of connotations for the people who use it: English as a *neutral language* and English as a *status language*. When bilingual or multilingual speakers change in the middle of a conversation to a different language, it may be that they want to emphasize different aspects either of the topic they are discussing or of their relationship with the person or persons they are talking to. A local language often has connotations of local cultural values and the feeling of intimacy. A non-English lingua franca may have connotations of belonging to a wider group or region. English, on the other hand, has connotations of education, socio-economic status and often also of power.[30] 'Those in authority', an educated Jamaican told us, 'talk English not Creole to their employees.' And from another part of the world, an educated Zambian commented:

> People who went to school and speak English consider themselves 'elite', upper class. . . . In Tanzania and Zambia people carry English newspapers just to be seen — even if they cannot read it [English] and hold them upside down.

CHAPTER 3

New accents

Probably the first impression that anyone has of a speaker of a New English is that he or she 'sounds different' or 'has a different accent'. If we say that someone has an *accent*, we usually mean that his or her way of speaking tells us something about this person. An accent may indicate what social class a speaker belongs to: 'She speaks with a working-class accent' or what region a speaker comes from: 'He has a slight Lancashire accent' or what country someone comes from: 'She has a very noticeable Australian accent.' People do not always judge other people's accents negatively — sometimes they find them attractive to listen to — sometimes just intriguingly different.

Of course, those varieties of English which have been spoken for a long time, the so-called 'native varieties', e.g. British English, American English, Australian English, Canadian English, New Zealand English, sound very different from one another. Within some of them, e.g. within British English or American English, there are further variations in speech according to the region where people come from.

The accents of the speakers of the New Englishes are different again from those of the more established varieties and are often in themselves quite distinct from one another. It is possible to say when one hears someone speak English: 'Oh, he sounds like a Singaporean', 'She could be a West African' or 'He sounds as if he comes from India.'

We do not want to say, of course, that the speech of all Singaporeans, West Africans or Indians sounds alike. In the last chapter, we have already mentioned that there are considerable variations according to the speakers' educational and often socio-economic backgrounds. In many countries, there are also regional differences which often show the influence of the local languages. In India, for instance, it is possible to talk of Bengali English, Hindi English, Panjabi English and Tamil English, in Nigeria of Hausa, Igbo and Yoruba English. However, in spite of all these educational and regional differences it is often possible to make certain generalizations about a New English.

In this chapter and the following chapters, we do not want to look at the language features of a particular New English in isolation. We want to see whether, in spite of the different language backgrounds of their speakers, there are not certain sounds, structures, patterns, strategies that are shared by some New Englishes even if they are spoken in areas which are geographically far apart.

Vowels

Naturally, there are many reasons why speakers of the New Englishes sound different. Let us look first at some of their vowel sounds. We must make a clear distinction between the printed or written letters of a word, for example the letter *a* in *cat* and the actual sounds that these letters represent. It is common to use symbols for these sounds and to put them in square brackets [ ] to distinguish them from letters. For example, in educated Southeastern British English (SBE) the letter *a* in *cat, fat, rat* would represent a sound for which we shall use the symbol [æ] but the letter *a* in *chance, dance, France* would represent the sound [ɑː]. In educated General American English (GAE), this is different and the *a* in *chance, dance, France* would also represent the sound [æ]. For those readers who wish to check up on the relationship between the most common sound symbols and printed letters, we have included a simple chart at the back of the book.

The way a vowel sound is heard depends very much on how wide the mouth is opened and on the position of the tongue in the mouth when the sound is pronounced. It also depends on the shape of the lips, whether they are rounded or whether they are spread. The tongue can have different positions in the mouth. The tip of the tongue can be raised or lowered, the back part of the tongue can be flat or raised. These all have their effect on the quality of a vowel.

For example, in SBE, the vowel sound in words like *calm* and *past* is pronounced with the tongue pulled back and bunched at the back and with the mouth fairly open. The sound is sometimes called a *back a* and represented by the symbol [ɑ]. In most of the New Englishes, the vowel sound in these words is pronounced with the tongue farther forward and more flat. This sound is sometimes called a *front a* and shown by the symbol [a]. It can be heard in words such as *father, calm, past, fast* in New Englishes spoken in places as far apart as Africa, Fiji, India, Sri Lanka, Papua New Guinea, Jamaica, Singapore and Malaysia. In Philippine English, because of American English influence, there is a variation between the front [a] and an [æ] sound for words such as *pass, class, fast*.

Of course, apart from quality, vowels may differ in length. If a vowel is long, like the sound in *past* (in SBE), the symbol has two dots after it, e.g. [pɑːst] *past*. In quite a number of the New Englishes, a length distinction is not always made. The sounds in *come* and *calm* are often the same and therefore the two words sound alike. The same goes for words such as *must* and *mast*. Sometimes there is some length but not nearly as much as in SBE. We shall use one dot after the vowel symbol to show this, e.g. [paˑs] *pass*.

When we asked a number of educated speakers of the New Englishes to read a list of words for us, we had the following pronunciations for the word *pass*:

		speakers from
long vowel	[paːs]	Papua New Guinea and Tanzania
some length	[paˑs]	Fiji, Ghana, Sri Lanka, Singapore
short	[pas]	India, Jamaica, Kenya, The Philippines and Uganda

But later on in reading passages and in conversations, speakers varied between longer and shorter [a] sounds for *pass* and similar words. Obviously there appears to be a general tendency in the New Englishes to make no regular distinction in vowel length and it is more common to have shorter vowel sounds than longer ones, except when a word is emphasized and then the vowel can be lengthened considerably, e.g.

I take de bus [baːs]

said by a Tanzanian speaker of English.

There are a number of vowels where the tip of the tongue is fairly far forward in the mouth. However, there are differences in how far forward the tongue is and how close it is to the roof of the mouth. Naturally, there are also differences in how far open the mouth is.

In some of the New Englishes, the tongue is raised higher and brought farther forward for the short *i*-sound in *sit* than it is in SBE and GAE.

For many speakers of Singapore English, for example, there is little difference in the pronunciation of such words as

sit   seat
this   these
rid   reed

although sometimes the vowel in *seat, these, reed* is slightly longer. This tendency can also be found in Indian English, Philippine English and the English of educated Papuans and New Guineans, e.g.

He used to bit (beat) me[1]

In the African Englishes too, there is often no distinction between the sounds in *bit* and *beat*. We have found that whilst some educated Africans make a distinction in length, others do not always make it, particularly not in fast, spontaneous speech. For example, educated speakers from Kenya, Malawi, Tanzania and Uganda varied between

speak pronounced with some length

    and

speak that sounded like SBE *spick* in *spick and span*

This lack of distinction can also be seen in written examples where the spelling of the word reflects African English pronunciation: From Ghana[2]

People will not seat (sit) down
Before I take my sit (seat)
So all and sundry enjoy leaving (living) in Ghana, even though the
    cost of leaving (living) is high.

From Tanzania[3]

By 1980, all expatriates are expected to live (leave) the country.
They will be replaced by Tanzanian experts who leave (live) here.

Some scholars claim that the reason for this lack of distinction in African English between long and short vowel sounds is that most African languages have relatively few contrasting vowels.[4] Many of the languages make no distinction between long and short vowels. Some, like Hausa, have a long [i:] sound only at the end of syllables. Others, like Fula, have distinctions between long and short [i] sounds but they differ in length only and not in vowel quality. It is interesting, however, that although some Africans have distinctions in their own language between long and short vowels, they seldom make this distinction when speaking English. For example, the Igbo language in Nigeria distinguishes between two types of *i*-sounds and two types of *u*-sounds but when Igbo speakers use English, they rarely make the *sheep/ship, fool/full* distinction. Angogo and Hancock[5] argue that there is a separate sound system in the African Englishes which speakers use no matter what their background languages.

In most New Englishes, the vowel sound in *hat, fat, rat* is different from that used in SBE and GAE. In some New Englishes, e.g. Singapore English, Malaysian English, Sri Lankan English and some of the Indian Englishes, there is a tendency to raise the tongue more, so that the vowel in *had* resembles that in *head*. For most speakers of Singapore English, for example, the vowels in these two words are identical. In communication across Englishes, it may cause some amusement, particularly if no distinction is made between final *d* and *t*, when someone is asked:

Take your head (hat) off and leave it in the hall

In many of the New Englishes, for example in the African Englishes, the vowel sound in *hat* and *had* is a front [a] sound. In spontaneous conversation, educated speakers from Kenya, Malawi, Uganda, Ghana and Nigeria used the same short front [a] in words like *had, have, act* as they did for *pass, past, fast*. The use of [a] in words like *had, have, act* is also typical for the various West Indian Englishes.[6]

In some of the older varieties of English, for example Australian English and some South African English, there is a tendency to pronounce many vowels with the tongue in a central position in the mouth and the mouth not very far open. The opposite is the case with many of the New Englishes. There is a definite tendency to avoid central vowels and to replace them by vowels which are either pronounced with the tongue farther forward in the mouth or farther back.

Let us have a quick look at the three vowels which are pronounced in SBE with the tongue more in the centre of the mouth. They are the short sound in *but*, the sound in *bird*, usually said with length, and a short *e*-sound which has the symbol [ə] (an *e* upside down) and occurs in unstressed syllables, e.g. in the first syllable of

about, allow, collapse, suppose

and in the last syllable of

actor, better, matter

In the African Englishes, for example, the last syllable in these words is usually pronounced with an [a] sound, e.g.

[mata]	*matter*
[bata]	*butter*
[visita]	*visitor*
[bia]	*beer*

The sound for *bird* varies. East African speakers of English are inclined to use an [a] sound[7] and West Africans an open *e*- sound [ɛ] or an *o*-sound [ɔ] with or without some length[8] but there is quite a noticeable regional variation. Jibril[9] shows that there is a difference between the Nigerian English spoken in the Northern states and that in the Southern states. He claims that the Southern states variety is considered to have more prestige in the country.

Northern Nigerian states	*Southern Nigerian states*
fur pronounced like far [fa]	*fur* pronounced like for [fɔ]
earn [aːn]	*earn* [aːn] or [ɛn]

The vowel in *but* differs too between the North and the South, e.g.

but [bat] in the North   and
but [bət] in the South

We have already mentioned that there is a tendency in many of the New Englishes to shorten vowels. There is also another factor. The longer the vowel, the harder it is to hold the tongue steady in one position. It slides up or down so that the second part of the vowel takes on the quality of another sound and instead of one vowel sound we really hear two sounds; one is usually more prominent than the other. For example, the vowel in *so* has two sound elements in many of the established varieties of English, and so has the vowel in *take*. Both vowels are referred to as *diphthongs*. It is a common feature of the New Englishes not only to shorten these vowels but to leave out one of the sound elements, usually the second one, e.g.

so

| Southeastern British English | səʊ | } | The second sound is usually represented by the short |
| General American English | soʊ | | u-sound [ʊ] |

35

New Englishes	so: so· sɔ	The short *u*-sound is missing

Southeastern British English and General American English	*take* teɪk	The second sound is usually represented by the short *i*- sound [ɪ]

New Englishes	te:(k) tɛ:(k) tɛ·(k) tɛ(k)	The short *i*-sound is missing

New Englishes with this tendency include Indian English,[10] Sri Lankan English,[11] Hong Kong English, Singapore and Malaysian English, African English and Papua New Guinean English.

We have already mentioned that vowel sounds can show what region a speaker of a New English comes from, e.g. whether he is from East or West Africa, even sometimes whether he comes from the Northern or Southern states of Nigeria. Sounds can also tell us something about the social and/or educational background of the speaker. Among other criteria, the length and the quality of the *o*-sound of *boat, road*, etc. may show the difference in Sri Lankan English[12] between

more educated speakers   [bo:t]   *boat*

       and

less educated speakers   [bɔt]   *boat*

Among Singaporeans with English-medium education, the higher a speaker's educational and socio-economic background, the more likely he or she will be to pronounce the second sound element, the *i*-element, in words like *take, rate, late*, and to lengthen the first element, e.g.

higher educational level and social status	eᴵ
	ɛᴵ
	ɛ:
lower educational level and social status	ɛ·
	ɛ

Summary

Summing up, we can see that there are some general tendencies which are shared by some or all of the New Englishes:

(1) a tendency to shorten vowel sounds;
(2) a lack of distinction between long and short vowels;
(3) a tendency to replace central vowels by either front or back vowels;
(4) a tendency to shorten diphthongs and to leave out the second sound element in a diphthong.

Distinctive sound units

We have already seen that there are some vowels in SBE which can change the meaning of a word if one is replaced by the other one, e.g. the short sound [ɪ] in *live* and the long sound [i:] in *leave*. It makes a difference, for instance, whether someone says about his wife's mother

> *I hope she'll live*   or
> *I hope she'll leave*

Every language has a group of sounds which are important to that language. They are used to form words in that particular language and, as we have seen with the vowels in *live* and *leave* in SBE, they often change the meaning of a word when they are replaced by another sound. It is claimed by psychologists and linguists that the speakers of a particular language or dialect have a system of distinctive sound units, sometimes referred to as *phonemes* or *phonemic units*, in their minds.

Consonants

Two sounds which are distinctive sounds in SBE and GAE are both written *th* and are pronounced with the tip of the tongue between the teeth. The air from the lungs is not stopped completely but allowed to escape with friction. This is why both sounds are called *fricatives*. One of them, the first sound in *thick, throw, thud*, is pronounced without vibration of the vocal cords. Its symbol is [θ]. The other sound, the first sound in words like *this, the, that*, is pronounced with the vocal cords vibrating. Its symbol is [ð]. To feel the difference between a

37

sound where the vocal cords are vibrating (a voiced sound) and a sound where the vocal cords are not vibrating (a voiceless sound) one can press one's fingers slightly against the front of one's neck. With voiced sounds a slight vibration can be felt.

In most of the New Englishes other sounds are often used instead of the two fricative sounds we have discussed. Often [d] is used in words like *the, this, that* and [t] in words like *thick* and *Thursday*. In Indian English, for example [d] and [t] in these words are pronounced with the tip of the tongue against the upper front teeth followed by a slight puff of air after them.[13] The use of [d] for [ð] and [t] for [θ] also occurs in Sri Lankan English, West Indian English and with some speakers of African Englishes so that

  den and *then*
  tick and *thick*

sound alike.

Teachers and linguists have asked themselves why substitutions like this take place. One of the theories which tries to account for it is called the theory of *contrastive linguistics*. It suggests that if someone acquires a new language which has a different sound system from his own, then he will be inclined to use sounds from his own system. Speakers would be particularly inclined to do this if the system of the new language had sounds that were not in their own language. They would then use sounds from their own language which are pronounced in the same or a similar position in the mouth, in this case either [d] and [t] or [z] and [s]. We have already discussed the use of [d] and [t]. Substitution by [z] and [s] is not as frequent in the New Englishes but it sometimes occurs, e.g.

  sing instead of *thing*
  ze instead of *the*

However, contrastive theory cannot always explain why speakers who have [d] and [t] as well as [z] and [s] in their own language use one pair rather than the other pair for the first sounds in *this* and *thick*.

Some speakers of New Englishes first make a [d] or [t] sound and then apply some friction after it, e.g. for some speakers of Malaysian English, Sri Lankan English, Singapore English and African English

  [dð] for the first sound in
    this, that, there

[tθ] for the first sound in
think, Thursday, thick

Cases such as these may be considered as learning strategies or verbal strategies which were used by the earlier speakers of these New Englishes. They tried to acquire the fricative and obtained only an approximation of it. Later on, other speakers of that New English may have imitated these sounds. This would be the case, particularly, if the earlier local speakers became teachers of English. After all, teachers are often important models for children in the areas where the New Englishes are spoken. We shall talk about this important factor of teacher influence in more detail in Chapter 10.

Naturally, there are many other differences in the use of consonants in the New Englishes. In Sri Lankan English and some of the Indian Englishes, for example, no distinction is made by most speakers between /v/ and /w/, e.g. *vell* (well).

A feature of less-educated speakers of Hong Kong English is the use of an *s*- sound for *sh* and *s* in words such as *should, sure, insurance*. This occurs also in some East African English, where the background language of the speakers does not use *sh*. dhoLuo speakers, for example, say [suga] *sugar* and [sat] *shut*.[14]

Sometimes the pronunciation depends on whether a consonant is at the beginning, the middle or the end of a word. In many of the New Englishes *p, t, k*, at the beginning of a word are pronounced without a puff of air (without aspiration). For instance the *t* in *time*, sounds like something between a [t] and a [d] sound. This happens, for example, in Indian, Sri Lankan, Singapore, Malaysian, Hong Kong and Philippine English. Words like

ten	and	*den*
pair	and	*bear*
pig	and	*big*

sound very similar. Sometimes, as in Philippine English, the distinction between these pairs of words becomes more noticeable in formal speech.

In some of the New Englishes, the [h] sound at the beginning of a word is sometimes used and sometimes not, e.g.

[ad]	or	[had]	for *had*
[əˑm]	or	[həˑm]	for *home*

(speakers from East Africa and Papua New Guinea)

Wells[15] mentions that in Jamaican English this variation is more noticeable in colloquial speech than in formal speech.

There are many ways in which final consonants can be pronounced. They can be voiceless, e.g.

in SBE [t] in *kit*

of they can be voiced, e.g.

in SBE [d] in *kid*

Sounds like [p, b, t, d, k, g] may be *unreleased*. For example, when pronouncing a [t] at the end of a word, the tongue is not immediately taken away from its position behind the teeth or the gum ridge. An unreleased [t] often sounds as if no [t] sound has been made at all, e.g.

ki(t)

Instead of some of the final consonants a *glottal stop* may be used. When making a glottal stop the air is stopped in the throat by constricting the throat slightly. This sound can be heard in some varieties of British English, e.g. Cockney English spoken in Inner London.

It is quite common in the New Englishes, for example in West African English[16] and Papua New Guinean English, to use a voiceless consonant at the end of words such as *read, proud, married, save, five, robe*, so that

read may sound like *writ*

and

married like *merit*

In Indian English, for example, the plural ending is usually an [s] sound even on words where [z] is used in other varieties of English, e.g. in *bees, bags, dogs*. On the other hand, speakers of Indian English[17] often use a [d] sound in past tense forms of verbs where other varieties would use a [t], e.g. *traced, developed, packed*. This may have been influenced by the way the words are spelt.

In some of the New Englishes, final consonants are often unreleased. This also occurs, of course, in other more established varieties of English. In SBE it is more common at the end of phrases or clauses, e.g.

He sat on her ha(t)
She hit him over the hea(d)

In some of the New Englishes, however, words with unreleased final consonants can occur anywhere in an utterance, e.g.

an(d) writing and grammar is qui(te) differen(t)

said by an educated Ghanaian.

Our research in Singapore has shown that in Singapore English, speakers usually vary between released and unreleased final consonants. In colloquial Singapore English and in the speech of those with lower levels of education, there is usually a variation between unreleased final consonants and replacement of consonants such as [p, t, k] by glottal stops. In the following examples, a letter in brackets means an unreleased stop, a ' means a glottal stop:

speaker 1   They pi' me u(p) a(t) seven
speaker 2   They pi' me u(p) a' seven
speaker 3   They pi' me u' a' seven
                (They pick me up at seven)

Using glottal stops for final *t* and sometimes for *p* and *k* is also common in Barbados English, a West Indian English,[18] e.g.

bi' – *bit*
ba' – *back*

A lack of distinction between /l/ and /r/ is not very common in the New Englishes. If it does occur, it usually tells us something about the speaker's regional or educational background. For example, speakers of East African languages such as Embu and Gikuyu will transfer the lack of distinction between these two sounds from their background languages to their English.[19] For example, there may be no distinction between words such as

light and *right*
belly and *berry*

The same can be noticed in the English of Chinese-medium educated Hong Kong or Singapore Chinese, e.g.

Engrish (English)   *correge* (college)

As with more established varieties, the New Englishes differ very much in the extent to which they make use of /r/ in words like *cart, part, clever, better* and what type of /r/ their speakers use. SBE does not have an /r/ in the above words – GAE has one. The frequency with which it is used can have a considerable effect on the way a New English sounds to a listener.

Many speakers of Indian English use it after a vowel in words like

port, here, better

To produce this /r/, they turn the tip of the tongue back to make slight contact with the roof of the mouth. They are also inclined to turn the tip of the tongue back when pronouncing [t] and [d]. Sounds which are produced in this way are called *retroflex*. Retroflex sounds give Indian English, particularly as spoken in Southern India, one of its very distinctive qualities.[20]

Philippine English, which has had American English as its norm, often makes use of retroflex /r/ in more formal speech but uses another /r/ which is sometimes called a *tap* in more colloquial speech.[21] In the tapped /r/, the tip of the tongue is tapped quickly against the gum ridge behind the upper front teeth.

In West Indian English, the use of /r/ varies between different areas.[22] In Trinidad, and most of the Windward and Leeward islands and the Bahamas, /r/ is not used in words such as *star, beer, four*, e.g. [sta] *star*. This distinguishes the English of these areas from that of Jamaica, Guyana and Barbados where an /r/ is used in these words. However, in Barbados English, the /r/ is used in *all* positions after vowels, e.g. in words such as

star and *start*
bear and *beard*

whereas in Jamaican English, the *start, beard* words usually have an /r/ in the more formal speech of educated speakers, but do not have it in colloquial speech.

Summary

Summing up, we can see that there are general tendencies which are shared by some or all of the New Englishes:

(1) replacement of the fricatives [ð] and [θ] by other sounds, usually [d] and [t] on their own or followed by slight friction;
(2) a tendency to make no distinction between certain voiced and voiceless consonants;

(3) a tendency to reduce the aspiration of consonants at the beginning of words;
(4) a tendency not to release consonants at the end of words.

Consonant groups

Languages vary considerably in their arrangements of consonants and vowels within a word. Some languages may have only one consonant at the beginning of a word, some not more than two. However, English is among the languages which may have some groups, or clusters, of three e.g. *str* in *street*. Some languages have no consonants at the end of words or only single consonants, some have clusters of two, whereas in others, such as English, three consonants may occur at the end of a word, e.g. *pints, risks, dialects, against*. Usually there are restrictions as to which consonants of a particular language may occur together in such clusters.

Various verbal strategies are apparent in the New Englishes for dealing with such consonant groups. Consonant clusters at the beginning may be split up by the addition of a vowel. The vowel is usually a short *e*-sound or an *i*-sound. This occurs at times in Indian English,[23] e.g.

[gəlas] *glass*
[pəlai] *play*

and in West and East African English, especially where [n] is one of the consonants, e.g. *against* is pronounced as if it were written *againest* and response as if it were written *responis*.[24]

In some New Englishes, e.g. Trinidadian English, a West-Indian English, consonant clusters at the beginning of a word are simplified by leaving out one of the consonants, e.g. [r] or [t].[25]

probably   *pobably*
from   *fom*
still   *sill*

In consonant clusters at the end of words, there is a tendency in many of the New Englishes not to pronounce the final consonant in a group of two, e.g.

last(t), mus(t)

or the middle or final consonant in a group of three, e.g.

dialec(t)s	or	*dialect(s)*
even(t)s	or	*event(s)*
wor(k)s	or	*work(s)*

This occurs, for instance, in the speech of Indians, Jamaicans, East and West Africans, Sri Lankans, Singaporeans and Malaysians.

Of course, in rapid speech, speakers of SBE and GAE would pronounce the middle consonant in a cluster of three or a final consonant in a cluster of two only slightly, but usually a trace of it can still be heard. In the New Englishes, it is often not heard at all.

Sey[26] who comments on this tendency in Ghanaian English, e.g. in words like

[pas]	*past*	[mis]	*mist*
[po:s]	*post*	[tɛːn]	*tend*

mentions that in a few cases it appears even in the written language, e.g.

past written *pass*:	*exactly half pass nine*
and *tend* written *turn*:	*...they turn to become paupers*
	...but turn to be selfish

In Singapore, the background languages of most speakers, that is Malay and the Southern Chinese dialects, do not have a cluster of two or three consonants at the end of words. In Singapore English, nearly all the speakers, particularly in informal speech, reduce clusters of three consonants at the end of words to two, e.g. *paren(t)s*. Reduction occurs more often in the speech of those with lower levels of education. These speakers frequently use only one consonant, e.g. *paren(ts)*.

Our investigation of variable use of two consonant clusters[27] at the end of words showed that there was a considerable difference. In the recorded spontaneous speech of a group of Singaporeans, those with high social status and educational level reduced clusters at the end of words like

just, recent, friend

only at an average of 12 per cent whereas for those with a low educational level and low socio-economic status, the average reduction was about 98 per cent. This means that for every 100 words which ended in groups of two consonants, these speakers used only one final consonant for 98 of the words, e.g.

jus(*t*), *recen*(*t*), *frien*(*d*)

Variable use

We have already mentioned that in all language varieties, whether they are native, near native or second language varieties, speakers vary considerably in their pronunciation. There is not only the difference between speakers of certain regions or social classes but also between speakers of the same region or the same class. There are also variations in the speech of an individual speaker. These can be noticed not only when comparing a speaker's formal and informal speech but also in the same passage of speech. Wells[28] illustrates this type of variation in short passages of spoken British and American English.

If a language feature, such as a sound, is used at some times and not at other times, it is referred to as *variable use*. The study of variable use of features in a language, e.g. the variable use of sounds, is of great importance. It presents a truer picture of what really goes on in speech than saying that a certain vowel or consonant is *always* used or that it is *not used* at all. Naturally, detailed investigations of variable use are time-consuming. In the case of speech sounds it involves the sampling of passages of spoken, preferably spontaneous speech, from a number of speakers. If this is done, some very interesting patterns emerge as can be seen from our occasional reference to our work on variation in Singapore English.

CHAPTER 4

One or more and other problems

When we talk or write about things, ideas or people, we usually make certain distinctions. We may indicate whether we are referring to one person or thing or to several. We may also wish to show whether these things, ideas or people are likely to be known already or are being mentioned for the first time. Often it is necessary to give more details about them or show their location in relation to the speaker or writer. In this chapter, we shall consider the class of words which refer to people, things and ideas, the nouns of a language, and some of the concepts which are closely associated with them.

Plurality

Languages may differ considerably in the way they show whether there is one of a kind or whether there are several; in other words how they show plurality.

In some languages, plurality is usually implied from the context. For example in Chinese (Mandarin):

Yǒu qiānbǐ méi yǒu?   Do you have pencils?
have pencil not have

Qiānbǐ, gāngbǐ, máobǐ – wǒmen dōu yǒu.
pencil   fountain pen writing brush – we all have
Pencils, fountain pens, writing brushes – we have them all

Other languages show that there are more than one by repeating the noun unless there is a number or another word or expression which shows quantity. For example in Malay:

bunga-bunga   flowers

    but

banyak bunga   many flowers

Others change the form of the noun to show plurality, e.g. in Swahili:

kitabu   book
vitabu   books

and others again add endings to nouns. For example, in English, the plural is normally formed by adding *-s* or *-es* in writing and [s], [z] or [ɪz] in speech:

pots, bins, classes

In many of the New Englishes, speakers do not always mark nouns for plurality by adding plural endings. They use the singular form of the noun, even if it follows a number or some other expression which means more than one. This can be seen in New Englishes from countries as far apart as India, Jamaica, the Philippines, Sri Lanka, Hong Kong and Singapore, e.g.

Most of the studen(ts) use to use Hindi medium only (India)

. . . up to twelve year(s) of schooling (India)

. . . and they know all four dialect(s) (Jamaica)

Pilipino is only one of the subject(s) (Philippines)

A province will be divided into district(s) (Philippines)

In both area(s) you get in English also (Sri Lanka)

Port Moresby University is for academic subject(s) (Papua New Guinea)

Sometimes, a speaker does not mark the plural, even if someone else has just used the plural form, e.g.

Q: These are called church schools?
A: Church school(s), ya. (speaker from Hong Kong)

and

Q: How many brothers and sisters do you have?
A: I got four brother(s), two sister(s). (speaker from Singapore)

Why do speakers of the New Englishes frequently not mark nouns for plural? There could be a number of reasons for this:

(1)   It may have something to do with pronunciation. We have already seen in chapter 3 that many of the background languages of speakers of the New Englishes do not have groups of consonants at the end of words. Very few have one or two consonants followed by an [s] or [z] sound as we can find in English words such as:

cups, tourists, risks, subjects

There is a tendency to pronounce only one consonant of a group of two, or one or two of a group of three. The one that is not pronounced may be the [s] or [z] sound which marks the plural. This may be *one* of the reasons for speakers frequently not marking the plural in Singapore English. The following examples are from the speech of educated Singaporeans:

There are quite a lot of active adult *educationist(s)*

I know people who speak with those *accent(s)*

Sometimes, of course, another consonant in the group may be left out and not the plural ending. Both examples below are from the same speaker of Indian English:

English is one of the subject(s)

English is one of the subjec(t)s

When the plural in English is shown by a change in the vowel, e.g. *foot – feet*, some speakers of New Englishes are more inclined to use the plural form. For example:

Come and wash your feet and hand(s)

said by a Malaysian mother to her children.

If plural endings are added at all to the noun, the voiceless [s] sound is used in many of the New Englishes where the voiced [z] is used in SBE and GAE, e.g. in words like:

bags, pens and *fans*

We have already commented on this in Chapter 3 when we talked about Indian English.

(2)   There may be interference from the way the speaker's background

language handles the concept of plurality. In Hokkien, a Chinese dialect understood and spoken by most Chinese in Singapore, plurality is inferred from the context:

Gua lang   si   chhâi-hông   We are tailors
  I people BE tailor

The fact that there is more than one tailor is implied by the plural subject *gua lang* 'we'. This comes through in the English of some Singaporeans, e.g.

We are still a student

Here the plural is implied because of the use of 'we'. It would seem that in the mind of the speaker each person who is covered by the 'we' is a student.

It is interesting that speakers of the New Englishes mark nouns for plural at certain times and not at other times. This is found to be true not only in speech, as the following example of colloquial Singapore English shows:

I buy dis New Year *thing*(*s*), like *flowers* like dis ah,
orange(*s*) ah, and dis *sweets*

but also in written and printed English. The following are from an order taken by a Singapore shop assistant:[1]

oranges
apple
pear   ?
bananas
grape ?
he pay Monday

and from a Jamaican newspaper article:[2]

. . .the Fourth Formers had written a letter to the School Board with a number of students' *name* signed to it.

. . .some students said they were shamefully driven through the *gates* of the school and the *gate* locked behind them.

It is common in some New Englishes to mark the plural of the noun more often in writing and in more formal speech. There would be less marking in colloquial speech. The common pattern is that the degree of noun plural marking is low for those with very little English-medium education but gets increasingly higher for those who have had higher levels of education. It was found that in an investigation of noun plural marking in Singapore English by one of the writers[3] the degree of marking the noun for plural fluctuated between 29 per cent for those with only primary education and 91 per cent for those with tertiary education.

However, nouns are sometimes marked for plural in the New Englishes where they would not be marked in the established varieties of English, e.g.

You see local *writings* say for a shop, the name of a shop or a restaurant   (an educated speaker from Ghana)

All our *rices* we have to import.

(an educated speaker from Hong Kong)

This tendency can also be noticed in the written language of the New Englishes, e.g.

from Papua New Guinea:[4]

I began to enjoy the *funs* we made

We have too many *works* to do

One day I packed up my *gears*

from Nigeria:[5]

I lost all my *furnitures* and valuable *properties*

Have you found any new *slangs* recently?

from the Philippines:[6]

He has many gray *hairs*

He has many *luggages*

This tendency is sometimes referred to as *overgeneralization*. What is meant by overgeneralization is that people acquiring a new language apply a rule too widely. In this case it would mean that they mark a noun for plural whenever it refers to more than one thing or person.

We feel that what is often called overgeneralization is really a type of reclassification. Many speakers and writers of the New Englishes appear to reclassify certain nouns which in more established varieties of English are considered to be uncountable nouns, e.g.

damage	→	damages
equipment	→	equipments
fruit	→	fruits
furniture	→	furnitures
machinery	→	machineries
staff	→	staffs
work	→	works

Of course, some of these, such as *damages* and *works*, do appear in their plural form in the more established varieties of English, but only in certain contexts, e.g.

He was awarded $50,000 damages.

The reasons for this reclassification could be:

(1) That speakers of the New Englishes have heard or seen some of these nouns in a context where they were used as count nouns, e.g.

He told us of his many unpleasant *experiences* at school

The kindly *fruits* of the earth (Book of Common Prayer)

(2) That speakers of the New Englishes consider that many of these nouns refer to separate items, so that *furniture* means *an item of furniture*, e.g. a table is *a furniture* and so is a chair. An apple, an orange or a banana is *a fruit*. Some of these words often appear in the singular in some of the New Englishes, sometimes preceded by an article, e.g.

from Singapore English:

(in the library) A *staff* came up to help us

This is a — more or less is a family concern here, you see. Excep(t) I got only one *staff* working wi(th) my father.

(3) A number of these nouns which refer to a collection of items are noticeably related to count nouns as the list below shows:

machinery	—	machines
scenery	—	scenes
jewellery	—	jewels

while others are cover terms for a group of countable nouns:

fruit   –   apples, pears, bananas, mangoes
aircraft   –   jumbo jets, helicopters, fighter planes
luggage   –   bags, suitcases

There are, however, nouns which would rarely appear in the plural in the New Englishes. Sey,[7] when talking about Ghanaian English, mentions that few educated Ghanaians would use words such as *mud*, *gold*, *petrol* in the plural form. We feel that this is because they are truly uncountable. They are usually thought of as a mass without any clear boundaries.

Some scholars have tried to explain this tendency as mainly an interference from the background languages.[8] However, there are background languages where these nouns are treated as uncountable nouns and yet the speakers still use plural forms for their equivalents in English.

In a few cases, the use of a plural form in a New English can be explained by the fact that there are two parts, e.g. the use of:

bottoms, bums, laps

in East African English[9] and in Singapore English. This would also apply to the East African use of *noses* in expressions such as:

my noses are stuffed up

An interesting example is *nighties* which is used in its plural form in a number of New Englishes for a singular item, e.g.

I was wearing my nighties when three visitors showed up[9]

This use of *nighties* was, no doubt, influenced by another type of 'night garment' – *pyjamas* which is always used in the plural.

Definite versus specific

It can often be noticed that in the New Englishes the rules for the use or non-use of the definite article *the* and the indefinite article *a (an)* are different from those in the more established varieties of English. Some people have simply tried to explain this as 'mistakes' or 'learners' errors'. We feel that this is an oversimplification of what has really occurred.

In order to understand what is happening, we need to look at two pairs of concepts:

(a)   definite and indefinite
(b)   specific and non-specific

English makes use of a *definite-indefinite* system. The definite concept is expressed by the use of the definite article *the* before singular and plural nouns:

the book   —   the books

and the indefinite concept by the use of *a(an)* before singular nouns and no article at all before plural nouns:

a rose   —   roses

What do we mean by definite and indefinite? These terms are frequently used in grammars but it is not always made clear *why* a noun or noun phrase should be considered as definite or indefinite. We have set out the main differences between the two concepts in Table 5.[10]

Table 5

(I) Definite	(II) Indefinite
The persons, things, etc. are thought by the speaker or writer to be *known* to the listener because	The persons, things, etc. are thought by the speaker or writer to be *unknown* to the listener or reader because
1 He has come across them before, e.g. *THE girl who rang you yesterday was my secretary*	1 He or she has not come across them before, e.g. *I'll tell you about A nice restaurant we went to yesterday*
2 There is (or is thought to be) only one of them in the universe, e.g. *THE sun is rising*	2 No *particular* person, thing, etc. is referred to, e.g. *Fred wants A job* (any job)
3 There is (or is thought to be) only one of them in the particular context, e.g. *Let's go to THE park* (There is only one park in the town, district, nearby)	*I couldn't find A seat* (any seat at all)
4 Because they belong to a known group or species, e.g. *THE penguin is a flightless bird.*	

One or more and other problems

Some languages, however, do not make a definite – indefinite distinction but rather a specific – non-specific distinction. Table 6 shows the main differences between specific and non-specific.[11]

Table 6

(I) Specific	(II) Non-specific
The persons, things, etc. are thought by the speaker or writer either (1) to have been previously *unknown* to the listener or reader, e.g. *he get WAN black buk* He has a black book (from Hawaiian Creole) or (2) to have been previously *known* to the listener or reader, e.g. *Jan bai DI buk* John bought the book (meaning a particular book which has been mentioned before) (from Guyana Creole)	(1) The persons, things, etc. are unknown to the speaker or writer *or* the identity of the item is thought by him to be irrelevant to the issue he is discussing *or* is thought to be obvious, e.g. *Jan bai buk* John bought a book (it is the book-buying that matters and it is not relevant here whether one or more or which book was bought) (from Guyana Creole) (2) The persons, things, etc. are not particular ones but belong to a group, type or species *dag smat* The dog (that is the species dog) is smart (from Hawaiian Creole)

We can see from Tables 5 and 6 that the main distinction between *definite* and *indefinite* is *known: not known* whereas the main distinction between *specific* and *non-specific* is *particular: not particular*. Within the specific concept there is often a further division into *known: not known*. The diagram on p. 55 shows the difference.

A number of long-established languages, e.g. Chinese, make the *specific/non-specific* distinction rather than the *definite/indefinite* distinction which English makes. Many of the New Englishes too appear to make the specific/non-specific distinction rather than follow the definite/indefinite division of the more established Englishes.

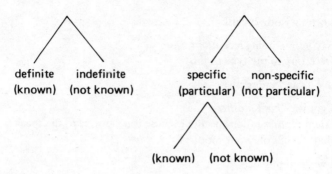

Non-specific

When the person or thing discussed or written about is non-specific (Table 6 II), often no article is used, e.g.

from Indian English:

> It looks like *cat*[12]
> (It belongs to the species cat)

> Everyone has *car*
> (No particular car or cars are being discussed)

> I really want to spend some time in *village*, definitely if I get *chance*.
> (Here no particular village is meant — just any village. The same goes for chance)

from West African English:

> . . .like *mudbrick* hut with *thatch roof*
> (not a particular hut but referring to a type of hut and a type of roof)

from East African English:

> I'm not on *scholarship*
> (not on any scholarship)

> So in *Tanzanian office* you'd be talking Swahili
> (not a particular office but any Tanzanian office)

from Papua New Guinean English:[13]

> I thought when I get *job* I will not be doing any more studies
> (The speaker didn't know what job he would be getting)

from Hong Kong English:[14]

> Say you're doing *receptionist job*
> (referring to the type of job)

from Singapore English:

> I got *very kind mother*
> (Here *mother* is non-specific because it is obvious to the speaker
> that she has only one mother)

> I want to buy *bag*

said by a Singapore student to his mother. In this case it is irrelevant
whether he wants to buy one only or another one for his friend. If he
had wished to specify that he intended to buy a particular bag, he would
most likely have said:

> I want to buy *one bag*

Specific

When the person or thing discussed or written about is specific, many
of the New Englishes make the distinction between *previously unknown* to the listener or reader and *previously known* to the listener
or reader (see Table 6 I). If the item is a particular one but unknown
to the listener, speakers of some of the New Englishes are inclined to
use *one* in front of singular nouns. This is particularly frequent in
colloquial speech. In the more established varieties of English, *one* is
usually used only when it is contrasted with *another* or *many*, e.g.

> I stayed with *one* friend for four days and then with *another* friend
> for a whole week

but in the New English examples below, no contrast is mentioned or
implied in the context. What the speaker refers to is a particular person
or thing that had previously been unknown to the listener and is mentioned for the first time, e.g.

from Indian English:

> I'm staying in *one house* with three other (students)

from Philippine English:

> *One old professor* was always inviting me to his house

from Malaysian English:

> Got *one boy*, morning also eat instant noodles, afternoon also eat instant noodles, night also eat instant noodles. Suddenly he died. The doctor found a lot of wax in his stomach.

from Singapore English:

> There! Here got *one stall* selling soup noodles

> Yesterday ah, seven something. I take *one passenger* to East Coast Road. . . .

> A: You share dress with your sister or not?
> B: No lah, I got *one whole wardrobe* my own what

If a person or thing is a particular one and if the speaker believes that the other person already knows of it, then it is common to use *the* in many of the New Englishes. In these cases there is an overlap with the definite concept of the definite/indefinite system of the more established varieties of English:

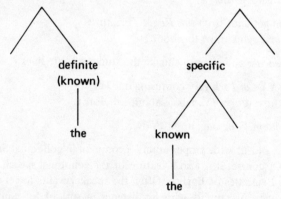

for example, from Singapore English:

> I diden(t) buy the dress lah
> (referring to a dress that has been discussed before)

In some New Englishes, *this/these* or *that/those* are also used for known specific items, e.g.

from colloquial Singapore English:

> *This handbag* you wanted to buy the other day. Buy already or not?

You diden(t) buy *this watch* ah — that one you wanted to buy
the other day?
(referring to a handbag or a watch that had been discussed before
but which need not be present. Here *this* has added the function
of aiding recollection of the object which is mentioned)

In British English, the expression *this handbag* would be used only
if the handbag was actually there to be pointed to, e.g.

A: I like your handbag. Where did you buy it?
B: This handbag? Oh I didn't buy it — George gave it to me

A possible reason for the use of the demonstrative in the New
Englishes instead of *the* could be that a number of the background
languages have no article forms. They always have demonstrative forms,
however. Although they may not be the exact equivalents to the
English *this/that/these/those*, the English demonstratives seem the
closest forms available to express something that is specific and known.
Further examples of *this/that* use for known specific items from
Singapore English are:

Ah, can get a lot from *this Roget Thesaurus*
(of course, you know this book)

That teacher ah, everytime make the students write lines

This XXX Car Park very confusing one lah
(you know it or we've talked about it before)

This Choon Fong rang up just now

The use of *this* with proper nouns is common in colloquial Singapore
English. Of course, it is also a feature of the colloquial speech of more
established varieties of English. Often the speaker wants to get a feeling
of immediacy or rapport with his listener, a sort of 'of course, you
know whom I've been talking about' or 'can't you just imagine it',
e.g. from Australian English:

. . . — and then *this Maggie Smith* comes along and wants me to give
her a lift

from British English:

This Joe Bloggs won't have much of a chance of keeping his seat
at the next election

The same desire to 'draw in the listener' may also underlie the use of *this* in some of the New Englishes.

There is often little distinction in pronunciation between *this* and *these*, both of which may be heard as [dis] or [dðis], e.g.

> . . . unlike *dis private schools* (an educated Nigerian)

> In my house I speak *all of dis languages* (an educated Tanzanian)

The difference between marking a 'specific and known item' (*this*) and a 'specific and not known item' (*one*) can be seen from the example below from Singapore English:

> You are going down to *this Ang Mo Kio Estate*, is it? From Bedok New Town there got *one bus* can take you straight there.

Naturally, not all speakers of all the New Englishes use a specific/ non-specific system *all* of the time. Some use it only sometimes, others not at all. Most speakers have been exposed to the rules of the definite/ indefinite system of British or American English in school or have come in contact with speakers of the more established varieties of English. Sometimes the two systems seem to operate side by side causing variable use of *the/this, a/one* or *a/zero* which can only be explained by a knowledge of both systems. In many cases, however, where people are inclined to talk about 'erratic mistakes', an application of specific/non-specific criteria would show up the system behind the apparent irregularities.

Quantifiers

Expressions which tell us about the number or amount of something are called *quantifiers*.[15] In British and American English, some expressions such as:

> *a few, a number, a couple, many*

are used with countable nouns, others such as:

> (*a*) *little, a great deal of, so much*

can be used only with uncountable nouns.

In the New Englishes, there is often no distinction in the use of these quantifiers, particularly in colloquial speech, e.g.

Don't eat *so much sweets*. Spoil your teeth! (Singapore English)

We try to get *as much word* across as possible (Malaysian English)

In expressions such as *a few, a number of, a couple of*, etc. *a* is frequently omitted in the New Englishes. The use of *a* seems incompatible with *few* and *couple* which are associated with the plural. Sometimes *a* is replaced by *some*, e.g.

from West African English:[16]

This money is given to the girl to buy *few articles*

I may continue with the interview or examine *few more applications*

X shot ahead in a field of 23 competitors *few minutes* from the start of the race

Some few minutes past nine I leave the office

Some few fishermen may be seen

from Indian English:

I applied *couple of places* in Australia

In X there are *number of schools*

I knew that he was coming *couple of months' time*

from Sri Lankan English:

You are expected to say *some few words*

They may use *few* (meaning *some*) of the Singhalese words

In communication between speakers of different varieties of English there would be no problem in understanding the meaning of these sentences except for the last one where the other meaning of few, that is 'less than expected' intrudes.

In some New Englishes, expressions such as *a (little) bit of* are reduced, particularly in colloquial speech, e.g. from Malaysian English:

I did *bit shopping*

Put *little bit five spice, little bit pepper, little bit salt* to give good flavour to the food

He got *little bit of knowledge* about acupuncture

Possession

Languages have many ways of showing possession. The English marking of a noun as a 'possessor' by adding *'s*, e.g.

my father's car

is often not used in the New Englishes, particularly not in colloquial speech, e.g.

this man brother (West Indian English)

women groups (Indian English)

children playground (Malaysian English)
(on a noticeboard)

Pronouns

We shall be looking at the use of pronouns in more detail in a later chapter. In general, the New Englishes use the same range of pronouns as the more established Englishes. In some New Englishes, however, where the background languages do not make a distinction between *he, she* and *it*, these are often used indiscriminately in the English of some of the speakers:

from East Africa:

My husband who was in England, *she* was by then my fiancé

When I first met my husband, *she* was a student

from Hong Kong:

(Someone was referring to her sister):
He work in office in Kowloon

from Malaysia:

My mother, *he* live in kampong

from Singapore:

(Someone referring to her son)
She born on national day

In Mandarin and the Chinese dialects only the written characters make a distinction between the male and female third-person pronoun:

他　　　　　male

她　　　　　female

The spoken forms do not make this distinction, e.g.

he/she	ta	–	Mandarin	some of the background
	i	–	Hokkien	languages for Singapore
	i	–	Hainanese	and Malaysian English
	koei	–	Cantonese	background language for
				Hong Kong English and some
				Singapore and Malaysian English

Adjectives

In English, forms of the verb may be used as adjectives, e.g.

verb stem + ing　　–　　a *fitting* remark

verb stem + ed　　–　　the *frayed* trousers

It is here that we find differences between the New Englishes and the more established varieties. In the following examples, the British English equivalent is in brackets:

from West African English:[17]

I find my daughter's behaviour *disgracing* (disgraceful)

Such arrangements are satisfactory and *justifying* (justified)

from Singapore English:

The instructions are very *complicating* (complicated)

A *matured* (mature) woman required to fill the position

You are most *welcomed* (welcome) to stay with us

from Malaysian English:

The museum will be *opened* (open) to the public between 10 a.m. – 6 p.m.

Word order

In the established Englishes, there is a definite and often complex order in which quantifiers, different types of adjectives and adjectival groups are placed before or after the noun.[18] This order is not always the same in the New Englishes, e.g.

These last two years	(British English)
Dis two last years	(Papua New Guinean English[19])
An exciting two-hour display	(British English)
A two hour exciting display	(Ghanaian English[20])

In some cases, the different word order in the New Englishes shows the influence of the background languages. For example in colloquial Singapore English, *all* may appear at the end of a noun group:

For Chinese New Year, we make jam tarts, jelly, love-letters *all* lah

This type of construction reflects structures from Mandarin and the Chinese dialects, e.g. Hokkien:

góa ê	láu-bú	tōa-chí	lóng-chóng	mē góa
My	mother	big sister	all	scold me

The same influence can be seen in constructions such as

Singapore/Malaysian English	*Hokkien*			
ninety over cheques	káu chảp	gōa	tiu^n	chi-phìo
	ninety	over	classifier	cheque
around two years plus	chha-put-to	nn̄g nî	gōa	
	approximately	two year	over	

In British English, for example, these constructions would be

over ninety cheques
over two years

An interesting case of background language influence *and* verbal strategy can be seen in certain word orders in Nigerian English. In Hausa, for example, the demonstrative precedes the noun but the possessive follows it:[21]

Wannan	littafi	naka
that	book	yours

In the English of Nigerians, the possessive often appears before the noun but *after* the demonstrative, e.g.[22]

... *that your* brother will he come?

... saying Amen to *those his* prayers

... to solve *this our* common problem

These constructions appear in the more established Englishes only in certain contexts, e.g. in the language of religion:

These our brethren...

In colloquial Singapore and Malaysian English, a combination of possessive and demonstrative may occur but the order is the reverse of that in Nigerian English. The possessive precedes the demonstrative, e.g.

Eh, *your this* plant very nice ah!

Your that brother come back already or not?

My that stupid brother, tell him how many times don't do – still do!

Conjoining

It is common in the colloquial speech of some of the New Englishes not to use conjunctions such as *and* when connecting nouns, e.g.

Altogether I have two brother, four sister (Singapore English)

It is also common not to use the conjunction *or* when connecting numerals, e.g.

five, six, seven years   (Singapore and Malaysian
four, five blocks away   English)

Of course, in these cases *or* is not meant to be a strong alternative but rather an estimate, and therefore no conjunction is used in some of the background languages.

Summary

To sum up, there are certain tendencies which are common to some or most of the New Englishes:

(1) a tendency not to mark nouns for plural;
(2) a tendency to use a specific/non-specific system for nouns rather than a definite/indefinite system, or to use the two systems side by side;
(3) a tendency to change the form of quantifiers;
(4) a tendency not to make a distinction between the third person pronouns *he* and *she*;
(5) a tendency to change the word order within the noun phrase.

CHAPTER 5

Actions, states and perceptions

Every language expresses in some way or other how people think, perceive and act, in what state people, things and ideas are and how they relate to each other. Words which express actions, states, perceptions etc., the verbs, occur in every language. However, there are many differences in the way they can be structured, what additional concepts they may express and what other words may occur with them.

Tense and aspect

Languages often have ways of showing whether an action took place in the past, will take place in the future or whether it generally takes place, e.g.

I went to town last Thursday

I think I'll go to town tomorrow

I go to town every day

Many languages also have ways of showing whether an action is going on at a particular time or whether it has finished, e.g.

He is mowing the lawn

He has just mown the lawn

The expression of past and future are generally considered to belong to a *tense system* and the completed action or ongoing action to an *aspect system.* This is a rather simplified division. Usually, the two systems are closely related and, as we shall see, there is considerable overlap.

Some languages have more complex systems of marking tenses and aspects than others. Some languages, e.g. Swahili,[1] also mark the verb to show whether the subject is I, you, he/she, etc. In English, except for the verb *be*, the only time the verb form is marked in any way to relate to the subject is in the third person singular, that is for a singular noun or he/she/it, e.g.

He still *lives* here

In a number of New Englishes, this *-s* marker on the verb form is not used regularly, particularly not in colloquial speech, e.g.

from Philippine English:[2]

He *go* to school

She *drink* milk

from Indian English:

Every microcosm *consist* of many cells

from East African English:

This *cater* for most of the students

If she *realize* that you are not following in English she switches to Swahili

In Singapore English, the verb is usually marked in the formal speech of educated speakers but is often unmarked in colloquial speech and the speech of less educated Singaporeans. When we analysed the speech of a group of English-medium educated Singaporeans with relatively low levels of education and lower status occupations, we found that the verb was marked for third person singular only at an average of 29 per cent.[3]

The non-marking of the verb form could, of course, be due to several factors. It may be that the background languages mark differently, e.g. Swahili, or not at all, e.g. the Chinese dialects. It could also be due to differences in pronunciation. For example, we have already mentioned in Chapter 3 that consonant groups at the end of a word are often reduced in the New Englishes, e.g.

last may be pronounced *las*

friends may be pronounced *friend* or *frien*
        and
he sits may be pronounced *he sit*

Differences in pronunciation may also sometimes be the cause when the verb is not marked in English for regular past tense, e.g.

Last year I *work* in Ipoh

However, as we shall see, there may be a number of other reasons why speakers of many of the New Englishes do not always mark verbs for past tense.

The following are examples from the colloquial speech of educated speakers of various New Englishes. In all of the cases, they referred to events in the past, e.g.

from Papua New Guinea:

(1) I *graduate* there in 1975

(2) Before *is* 5 years. Now they change it

from the Philippines:

(3) And then I *go* to the Public School

(4) Some of them crying because teacher *ask* them to read stories in Filipino

(5) I was new here and I *don't* know where to go

from India:

(6) And then I *look* in the Australian one (newspaper)

(7) I *move* to hostel

from East Africa:

(8) I *stay* with my brother

from Hong Kong:

(9) Mandarin, I *learn* it privately

from Singapore:

(10) My wife, she *pass* her Cambridge

(11) Last year I *stay* three months in Germany

(12) We *stay* there whole afternoon and we *catch* one small fish
      (laughter)

As can be seen, some of the examples of non-marking may be because in the background languages words do not end in final consonants
or groups of consonants. However, this would not explain *is* in example
(2), *go* in (3) *don't* in (5) and *catch* in (12).

As we said at the beginning of this chapter, there are two different
systems in relation to the verb. One, the *tense system*, shows the *time*,
e.g. whether or not something took place in the past. The other, the
aspect system, shows, for example, whether an action is finished or is
still going on. It is often claimed that English makes use of both
systems, e.g.

Billy washes cars to earn pocket money (TENSE: NON-PAST)

He washed our car yesterday   (TENSE: PAST)

He's washing Mrs Bowen's car now   (ASPECT: PROGRESSIVE)

But, Mum, I've already washed the car! (ASPECT: COMPLETIVE)

However, this is an oversimplified way of showing it. The two systems
are really more complex in English and closely interlocked.

In some of the background languages to the New Englishes, the
aspect system appears to be more important than the tense system.
For example, in Hausa, a West African language:[4]

na sani	I know/ I knew
na ji	I hear/ I heard
na gani	I see/ I saw

There is no need to mark the verb for tense, once the time of action has
been specified, e.g. by an adverb or adverbial phrase. This is often
transferred to West African English:[5]

(from the television speech of a Hausa speaker)

It was during that time these people *make* some arrangement with
law enforcement agencies. . . .

The use of adverbs of time instead of marking verbs for tense is
common too in other New Englishes, e.g.

from Malaysian English:

69

Before I always *go* to that market

from Singapore English:

Last time she *come* on Thursday

It is quite common to 'set the scene' by specifying that something took place in the past and then to use all the verbs unmarked for past tense. e.g.

When I small that time, I *stay* with my auntie. . .

Young that time I always *go* fishing. . .

Structures such as *when I small* and *young that time* have equivalents in the Southern Chinese dialects.

The Southern Chinese dialects and Malay, which are the main background languages for Singapore and Malaysian English, favour an aspect system rather than a tense system. For example in Malay, an ongoing action is shown by *sedang* (still, in the midst of):

saya sedang makan   I am/was eating
I   still   eat

A completed action is shown by *sudah* (completed, finished, already):

saya sudah makan   I have/had eaten
I   finish eat

but *saya makan* can mean *I eat* or *I ate*

In Hokkien, the main Southern Chinese dialect spoken in Singapore, an ongoing action in the present may be shown by *chit-chūn* (now) e.g.

Goá chit-chūn chú png   I'm cooking rice
I   now   cook rice

A completed action may be shown by liáu (finished already), e.g.

Goá chiáh pá liáu   I have finished eating
I   eat   full aready

Sometimes words such as other verbs or adverbs are used in the New Englishes to show certain aspects of an action. We can say that they are used like *aspect markers*. In colloquial Singapore and Malaysian English, *use to* marks habitual actions (often still going on), e.g.

My mother, she *use to* go to Pulau Tikus market
(meaning she still does so)

I *use to* converse with my amah in Cantonese
(meaning I talk Cantonese with our maid servant)

For a completed action, some New Englishes make use of short words, either from the background languages or from English. For example, in the English of the Philippine nursemaids, the *yayas*, completed action is sometimes shown by *na:* [6]

Matthew finish *na*
(meaning: Matthew has finished)

Na is sometimes used as an aspect marker in Pilipino, the national language of the Philippines.

In colloquial Singapore and Malaysian English, *already* is used to indicate completed actions and events, e.g.

My father *already* pass away
(My father has passed away, has died)

You finish makan *already?*
(Have you already eaten?)

However, *already* has another meaning in Singapore and Malaysian English, namely that of *any more*, as in

I don't drink coffee *already*

Another marker for completed action in Singapore and Malaysian English, particularly in very colloquial speech, is *finish*, e.g.

You *eat finish*, go out and play
(When you've finished eating, go and play outside)

For a number of speakers of the New Englishes, the English construction with *has/have been*, apart from suggesting a completed state or action, also strongly suggests a time element in the past, e.g.

from Indian English: [7]

I *have worked* there in 1960

I *have read* this book yesterday

from Philippine English: [8]

I *have seen* him yesterday

In this way, they often do not make use of the options that most varieties of British and American English have in focussing either on completion or on time, e.g.

(stressing completion)   But *I've seen* the film

(stressing time)   But I saw this film *last week*

An action that is going on at a particular time, either in the present or in the past, is often referred to as having a *durative aspect* or a progressive aspect as it has 'duration' or is in 'progress', e.g. in English:

I'm just typing your letter now, Mr Smith

I was typing the letter when he arrived

Sometimes New Englishes use verbs other than *be* to express this on-going action. For example in the colloquial speech of speakers of Hawaiian English, *stay* may be used:[9]

What you *stay* eat?
(What are you eating?)

A very noticeable feature of many of the New Englishes is that the *be* + *verb* + *ing* construction is extended to verbs which, in most varieties of British and American English, are not generally used in this form or which are used in *-ing* constructions only in certain contexts.

A division is sometimes made between verbs that describe a state, *stative verbs*, such as *be, have, like, doubt, know*, and those that describe an action, process, event, etc., the *non-stative verbs*. These latter verbs appear in *-ing* constructions in the more established varieties of English. However, in a number of the New Englishes, stative verbs, too, are often used in *-ing* constructions, e.g.

from Indian English:

Mohan *is having* two houses[10]

Ram *was knowing* that he would come[10]

I *was doubting* it

from Singapore English:

I *am having* a cold

She *is having* a headache

from Papua New Guinean English:[11]

We *are knowing* more about continuous tenses

Only a few of us *were having* this opportunity

from East African English:

She *is knowing* her science very well

from West African English:[12]

I *am doubting* whether he will come

He *is thinking* that he is stronger than everybody else

There may be various reasons for these constructions in the New Englishes. The extended use of *-ing* constructions may be due to the influence of the background languages. For example, in Nigerian and Ghanaian English, constructions such as *I am having a cold* may show the influence of the Kwa languages. Their aspect system makes a distinction between permanent states, such as *I have a body* and less permanent ones.[13] However, in other African languages such a distinction is not made and yet there is still an extension of *-ing* use.

One of the reasons may be 'overteaching'. At an early stage when the language was taught, teachers may have stressed the *-ing* form of the English verb as an essential part of the verbal system and therefore speakers began to use it with every English verb. There may also have been an over-extension from the use in more established varieties of English of such constructions as

I'*m having* a meal

She'*s having* a good time

where action and progress are implied.

An interesting case is the use of verbs such as *say* and *tell* in *-ing* constructions. In the British English sentence

He *told* me that he had sold his house

the focus is on the fact that he 'had sold his house' and not on the telling, but in

She *was telling* me over and over again

the focus is on the repetition and the process of *telling*. Speakers of New Englishes sometimes try to achieve this idea of repeated action or progression by using *tell* and *say* in *-ing* constructions e.g.

from Indian English:

> He *was telling* me that he can get it at half rate
> (apparently a rather lengthy or repeated *telling*)

from Philippine English:

> They *were saying* 'Why don't you join us watch TV'
> (apparently an offer repeatedly made)

There is at times a difference between the New Englishes and the more established Englishes in talking about future events. In colloquial speech, a number of New Englishes make use of *go*, e.g.

from Singapore English:

> I think I *go* and make one new dress for Chinese New Year

There is, in some New Englishes, the tendency to express events in the future, even the immediate future, by *will*. Sometimes, *will* is used where it is not certain whether the action will take place at all, e.g.

from Ghanaian English:[12]

> If I *will have* my way, I *will leave* this place now

> I *will like* to go right now

> I *will like* to see him

In other New Englishes, e.g. Singapore English, *would* is frequently used instead of *will* for future events. The following examples are from written or printed Singapore English:[14]

> If I can induce anger in at least one reader, this article *would have* more than served its purpose

> It is strongly hoped that the reserved lanes *would give* priority to public buses

> The advertisement in the paper says that the film *would begin* promptly at seven.

This use may be due to an attempt to sound more official or elegant.

The *would* or *had* (or their shortened form *'d*) are frequently not used in constructions such as *I'd better, I'd rather, I would like, I would prefer*, etc., e.g.

from Philippine English:[15]

I like some ice cream now

from Ghanaian English:[12]

I better leave now

from Malaysian English:

I rather go by plane

Better you don'(t) smoke here!

Better you don'(t) throw rubbish in Singapore! You must pay heavy fine, man!

As with other language features, speakers of the New Englishes sometimes mark verbs in English for tense and sometimes do not. It may depend on the situation, the style and the background of the speaker. We compared the speech of two groups of English-medium educated Singaporeans in order to see what difference there was in their marking of verbs for past tense.[16] Group I had higher-status occupations and an education beyond GCE (the Cambridge O-Level). Group II had lower-status occupations and had either GCE or less education. For example, for verbs that required a vowel change to form their past tense, such as

come   →   *came*

the percentages of marked verb forms were

Group I	Group II
91 per cent	55 per cent

For verbs which ended in a consonant and formed their past tense by adding a [t] or [d] sound in speech, such as *work → worked, rob → robbed,* the percentages of marked verb forms were

Group I	Group II
54 per cent	19 per cent

With these verbs, there is obviously some influence from pronunciation.

For example in speech, verb forms such as *worked, robbed, danced* end in a group of two or three consonants. As we mentioned in Chapter 3, these groups are often reduced.

It appears that in some of the New Englishes, it also matters whether a verb is used to describe a relatively short action or event at a point in time, the so-called *punctual* use of the verb, e.g.

She punched him on the nose

or whether it describes something that happened over a longer period of time or repeatedly, e.g.

My parents lived in Ipoh

Punctual verbs are more likely to be marked for past tense than non-punctual verbs. We carried out an investigation on the marking of past tense in the speech of a group of Singaporeans. They were all English-medium educated but had reached only lower levels of secondary school and were in lower-status occupations. Verbs which were used *punctually* were marked for the past tense 36 per cent of the time, whereas verbs which were used *non-punctually* were marked only 19 per cent of the time.[17] It is obvious that there is a greater tendency to specify the time factor for short actions and events.

An example of variable marking of verbs for tense and aspect can be seen from the following conversation between two Malaysians speaking English:

(A arrives at B's house)
A: Eh, where you go jus(t) now?
B: I diden go anywhere what. Want to makan now?
A: I just finish makan. I rang up 12 somet(h)ing. Not in ah?
B: No, in all the time what.
A: I rang up – so long nobody answer. I t(h)ought you wen(t) out already. No answer at all lah!
B: Maybe the line spoil or what, because I never hear the phone ring. OK lah, then I go and makan myself now. So hungry already!
A: Sorry lah! Eat together another time lah!

Negation

In order to avoid the use of *don't, didn't*, etc., some of the speakers of the New Englishes use *never* in colloquial speech, e.g.

from Hawaiian English:[18]

I nevah take that picture   'I didn't take. . .'

I nevah sleep today   'I haven't slept. . .'

He nevah come already   'He hasn't come yet'

from Singapore English:

Who say I take your book! I *never* take your book

In Australia, people *never* carry umbrella — so if you carry they will laugh at you

He *never* come already   'He doesn't come anymore'

Of course, *never* is also used for negation in some of the more established varieties by speakers of lower status and education, e.g. from British English and Australian English:

I never seen him

He never give it to me

As we have already mentioned in Chapter 3, in many of the New Englishes, groups of two or three consonants are avoided at the end of words. *Didn't, couldn't, wouldn't*, etc. become

diden, coulden, woulden

and *don't and can't* often become

don'(t)   [dɔn]   and
can'(t)   [ka:n]

For example from Philippine English:

I *coulden* describe how they speak

and from Singapore English:

He *diden* come yesterday

I *diden* receive a reply

Sometimes, *do* is used more frequently than in the more established Englishes, e.g. in Indian English,

Yes, we do have, we do call them intervals

We do have those so many good sweets

We do celebrate in two days

In each case, the speaker did not stress *do*.

BE

The verb *be* as a link between the subject and an adjective, noun, noun phrase, etc. is sometimes not used in the New Englishes, particularly not in colloquial speech, e.g.

from Singapore English:

This coffee house — very cheap

from Hong Kong English:

English — main language of instruction

from East African English:

This (pointing to a name on a sheet of paper) my dialect

from Indian English:

That — the second festival I'm going to tell you (about)

from Malaysian English:

My sister — in London

In a number of the background languages to the New Englishes, a linking verb between the subject and an adjective or noun is not essential as the meaning is obvious from the word order. In other languages a linking verb is used only for emphasis. For example, in most of the main background languages to Singapore and Malaysian English, the verb *be* is seldom used before adjectives, e.g.

(1) in the Southern Chinese dialects and Mandarin:

Goá chin hó	(Hokkien)	
Ngo hóu hóu	(Cantonese)	I'm very well
Wo hén haǒ	(Mandarin)	
I very well		

(2) in Bazaar Malay (spoken by some older Chinese and Indians in Singapore and Malaysia):

Saya punya   rumah banyak besar   My house is very big
I   (possessive) house very   big

(3) in Malay:

Rumahku besar sekali   My house is very big
House-my big   very

(4) in Tamil, the main Indian langauge spoken in Singapore and Malaysia:

In̪d̪ə sa:ppad̼u n̪elled̼u   This food is good
This food   good

It is not surprising then that in colloquial Singapore and Malaysian English the verb *be* is frequently not used, particularly not before adjectives. For a group of English-medium educated Singaporeans with lower levels of education it was found that forms of the verb *be* were used only 63 per cent of the time before adjectives.

In English passive constructions, such as:

They were smuggled out

speakers of the New Englishes do not always use forms of the verb *be*, e.g.

from Hong Kong English:

The Vietnam people – smuggle(d) out

from Philippine English:

The private schools – mostly run by religious orders

from Ghanaian English:

As soon as children are about 4 or 3 they – sent to Kinder

from Singapore English:

Pack your toy(s)! This room must – clean before Chinese New Year

Active/Passive

Some verbs in the New Englishes can have an active or a passive meaning, according to the context. The same construction is used. For example, in Singapore English:

You *can eat* this cake

> or

The seed(s) (of a certain fruit) *can eat*
(meaning *can be eaten* or *are edible*)

Can you buy dresses from Sim's Boutique?
Yah, the dresses from there *can wear*
(meaning 'The dresses can be worn by me' or 'The dresses fit me
or suit me')

We shall look more closely at the extended use of some verbs in Chapter 6 which deals with different ways of expressing meaning in the New Englishes.

Existence and location

There are expressions in English which show that something exists. Two constructions are often used. Although they do not look very similar they have a similarity in meaning:

There is a lot of room in this car

This car *has* a lot of room (in it)

In these cases, some of the New Englishes may also use forms of *get* in colloquial speech, e.g.

from Hawaiian English[19]

Q: Whose car get room?
A: That one *get*

from Singapore English:

This here coffeehouse *got* a lot of cockroach(es)

Also *got* customer(s) come in

Here got a lot of people come and eat

Phrasal and prepositional verbs

Combinations of verbs with particles and prepositions are very common in English. Usually, a distinction is made between two groups: *phrasal verbs* and *prepositional verbs.*[20] Phrasal verbs consist of a verb and a particle which is closely connected with the verb, e.g.

to drink up, to give in, to call off

They cannot be separated by adverbs but the particle may follow the direct object as long as the direct object is not too long, e.g.

They called off the strike

They called the strike off

Prepositional verbs are connected with a noun, noun phrase, etc. by a particular preposition, e.g.

to look at (something or someone)

These prepositions are *before* the noun or noun phrase, e.g.

They looked at the picture

but, unlike the phrasal verbs, an adverb may come between the verb and the preposition, e.g.

They looked closely at the picture

In many of the New Englishes, there are different phrasal and prepositional verb constructions. Phrasal verbs are used without particles or with different particles, new phrasal verbs are created, prepositional verbs are used with different prepositions or without prepositions. To condemn all this as 'deviant usage' or 'learners' errors' would be wrong, particularly if a construction is spread over New Englishes geographically as far apart as West Africa and Singapore. However, there is obviously a continuum ranging from constructions that are chosen haphazardly because of linguistic insecurity to those constructions that are a regular feature of a particular New English.

It would not be feasible to include all possible combinations here. We have concentrated on those which appear to be more frequently used and/or which are more widely spread throughout the various New Englishes. For convenience' sake, we have divided our examples into various subgroups. It must be realized, of course, that these constructions may not be used by *all* speakers of the New English and that some are used only in colloquial speech. Where we know that they have occurred in written language, they are marked by (WR) before the example. The term *English* used in some of the headings refers to the use in the more established varieties of English.

(1) *English phrasal verbs used without a particle*

from East African English:[21]

Her name *cropped* in the conversation

He *picked* him outside his house

from West African English:[22]

(WR) I stopped to *pick* my own suitcase and reported the matter to the Railway

from Singapore English:[23]

(WR) *Pick* me at seven from the bus stop. . .

(WR) Bowling alleys have recently been *sprouting* all over the city

(2) *English phrasal verbs used with a different particle*

from West African English:[22]

(WR) It took the combined team of the National Fire Service and the Armed Forces Fire Service. . .about two hours to *put off* the fire

from Hawaiian English:[24]

Poor baby — he *trow out* his milk
(The poor baby threw up his milk)

from Singapore English:

He *threw out* his hands in despair

(3) *Verbs used as phrasal verbs*

This means that a particle is used, often *up* or *out*, where there is none in the more established varieties of English.

from West African English:[25]

I'm going to *voice out* my opinion

The people suffer many hardships but they have no way to *voice* their feelings *out*

His shouts for help awoke the houseboy, but before the houseboy could open the door it had been *locked up* by the thugs:[22]

from Singapore English:

You can *voice out* what you are not satisfied with at the meeting

(4) *English prepositional verbs used without a preposition*

from Indian English:

I *applied* couple of places in Australia

from Singapore English:[26]

(WR)   Our mutual benefit schemes *provide* you and your family financial relief in emergencies

(5) *English prepositional verbs used with different prepositions*

from West African English:[27]

(WR)   Africa must prepare herself sufficiently for this last conflict which is even likely to *result into* a world war

(WR)   The idea of banning students' dances is like *depriving* a baby *from* his mother's breast

I *congratulate* you *for* your brilliant performance

from Hawaiian English:[28]

We drove this car and when we came down to Kukuihaele, we all *get down* and walk

This may be an influence from Korean *naerida* and Japanese *oriru* 'to go (come) down' used for getting out of a car and getting off a bus.

I *got on* the Ford, drove to town and got off

In similar constructions, the Hawaiian language uses *luna* 'on'. There may also have been an influence from Chinese, Japanese and Korean.

from Singapore English:

He *got up* the bus

He *got down* the bus

In colloquial Singapore Hokkien and Cantonese, these constructions
would be

Hokkien: i   khí   bas chhia   Cantonese: kŏei sĕong   bas chè
         He go up   bus   he   go up   bus
         i   lóh   bas chhia   kŏei lŏk   bas chè
         He go down bus   he   go down bus

An interesting case is the prepositional verb *to cope with* which is
used with the additional particle *up* in a number of the New Englishes,
e.g. from West African English:[29]

(WR)   Each and every day one was well informed to *cope up with*
        any eventuality

(WR)   . . .there should have been a corresponding increase in
        number of machines like tractors and combine harvesters
        to *cope up with* the situation

from Singapore English:

(WR)   An average person is able *to cope up with* training without
        undue stress

(6) *English non-prepositional verbs used with prepositions*

The most common prepositions used are *to, on, out* and *about*, e.g.
from West African English:[27]

We shall *discuss about* this later

(WR)   The High Commissioner also *stressed on* the importance of
        Ghanaian students registering their names and addresses
        with this office

from Papua New Guinean English:

We must *discuss about* this later

from Singapore English:[23]

(WR)   They *discussed about* the mistakes and *emphasized on* the
        need for greater care

There are a number of possible reasons to account for the differences in these verbs.[30] We have already mentioned possible influences from the background languages. On the other hand, a number of these constructions could be due to language strategies, e.g.

(1)   Analogy with similar verbs in English

speak out   —   voice *out*
consist of   —   comprise *of*
talk about   —   discuss *about*

(2)   With newly formed prepositional verbs, such as *discuss about* it is usual in the more established varieties of English for the related noun to take this particular preposition, e.g.

emphasize   — emphasis on   — emphasize *on*
discuss   — discussion about   — discuss *about*

(3)   The verb suggests the meaning of the preposition that is added in the New Englishes, e.g.

vomit out
vacate out   movement away from
remove out

(4)   Some constructions may be influenced by closely related verb forms, e.g.

pick/pick up
take/take up/take off
lock/lock up
speak up/speak out

Summary

To sum up, there are certain tendencies which are common to some or most of the New Englishes:

(1)   a tendency not to mark the verb for third person singular in its present-tense form;
(2)   a tendency not to mark verbs for the past tense. This tendency is stronger when verbs are used non-punctually;

(3) a tendency to use an aspect system rather than a tense system or to use both systems side by side;

(4) a tendency to extend the use of *be + verb + ing* constructions to stative verbs;

(5) the formation of different phrasal and prepositional verb constructions.

CHAPTER 6

New words and new meanings

When a new variety of a language develops, it does not develop in isolation but it depends on the communicative needs of those who speak it and write it. The type of English used in Britain, for example, may serve some of the communicative needs of a new nation but by no means all of them. It may lack words and phrases to express the cultural background of the people of the new nation, words which refer to local food, clothing, housing, festivals, words which reflect certain family relations or status relations, in fact a whole range of different social relationships. It may not have words or phrases which (accurately) express the thoughts and feelings of the people in the new nations, those thoughts and feelings which they were able to express adequately and forcefully in their own local languages.

The speakers of the New Englishes have developed and, in many cases, are still developing a whole new range of expressions to fulfil their communicative needs. Not all of these are 'new' creations. A variety of different language strategies have been at play. Words have been taken over from the background languages, new words have been created from existing English forms and existing English words have extended their meaning or even changed their meaning completely. Particularly in colloquial speech, colourful idiomatic expressions have appeared in many of the New Englishes. Some already existed in the background languages and have been translated into English, often word for word. Others did not exist in the local languages and are new creations. It is interesting that, in some cases, similar new creations appear in New Englishes which are geographically quite far apart.

Loan words from the background languages

Every language or language variety which has been in contact with
other languages has for some reason or other taken over words from
these other languages. The term *loan word* does not really seem a very
apt expression as it implies 'a return to the original owner' – whereas
these words have become part of the language that has adopted them.
The English language, for example, has a large number of loan words.
Some are centuries old – some relatively recent, e.g. *data* from Latin,
stigma from Greek, *coup d'état* from French, *blitz* from German.
Sometimes, speakers pronounce the loan words as they are pronounced
in the original language but gradually some of them become adapted
to the sound system of the new language. In the New Englishes, this
would be the case particularly for those speakers who use the New
English more than their local languages.

Of course, we do not want to imply that *all* words from the background languages which are used by the people speaking English in a
New Nation are *loan words*. There is usually in a New Nation a whole
range of speakers of different socio-economic and educational backgrounds having varying degrees of proficiency in the New English.
There are those whose knowledge of English is limited and who feel
more at ease when speaking their local languages. When speaking
English, they often lack the necessary English vocabulary to express
themselves adequately and use words from the local languages and
dialects in their English. These words cannot be considered loan words
of that New English as they are usually haphazardly chosen as the need
arises. (We shall talk about the deliberate mixing of two languages as a
stylistic device in a later chapter.) There are other words which are
used quite frequently by speakers who have had more English education.
They use these words because they feel that something they want to
say cannot be expressed in any other way. Maybe one should call these
words *loan words in the making*. The true loan words in the New
English would be those which were used or recognized by most of the
speakers as belonging to 'their variety of English'.

Figure 3 shows that there is, of course, at times a possibility that
haphazardly used words from a background language may slowly become stabilized loan words if they begin to fulfil a real need. However,
this is not always so. On the other hand, loan words which are in the
making and which we have in our diagram called *stabilizing loan words*
may, in time, become more firmly rooted in the New English.

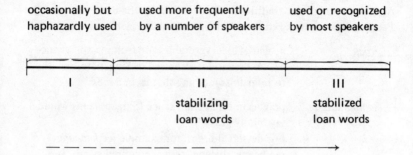

Figure 3 Words from background languages

Of the loan words which are stabilized, some would be used all the time, others may be used only in colloquial speech and others again may appear more frequently in speech than in writing.

There is a fourth group of words which are not used haphazardly but quite deliberately. Their users are the creative writers of the new nation who use words and expressions from the local languages to convey atmosphere, shades of meaning and experiences which are tightly bound up with local background cultures. We shall talk more about the use of New English in literature in chapter 11. Loan words or loan translations used in literature may gradually become stabilized loan words in a New English. However, this depends on the need they fulfil in the English-speaking community in the new nation as well as on the influence of the writer on his readers.

Our examples of loan words will be mainly from Group III. However, some Group II and even Group I words have been included as there is often no clear division between loan words which are still stabilizing and those which have been accepted by the majority of speakers.

An area where loan words from the New Englishes have become practically 'universal' is the area of food and cooking. Sophisticated hostesses, not only in English-speaking countries but all over the world, may prepare *sate* or *satay* 'spiced barbecued meat on sticks with a spicy sauce' (from Malaysia), *curry* and *mulligatawny* (from India) and *adobo* 'a meat stew' (from the Philippines). There are, of course, a number of words relating to food which are widely used in New Englishes in a particular area but less known among speakers of other varieties of English. For example, speakers of Singapore English would use terms which refer to Chinese food, Malay food and the tasty dishes of the

Nonya cooking, the traditional food of the Straits-born Chinese, the Peranakan, with its mixture of Chinese and Malay elements, e.g.

rojak	a salad of local vegetables and fruit in a spicy sauce The expression is also used in Singapore English to refer to something that is 'in a mess'
sambal udang	prawns in thick chilli sauce (Singaporeans would say 'chilly gravy') For dessert there is, for example *ice kachang*: red beans, shavings of ice, coloured syrup, and sweetened condensed milk as well as delicious little *nonya* cakes.

Food and shopping, clothing, housing, gardening and transport, all these areas of everyday activity have their share of loan words.

In colloquial Singapore English you 'take *makan*' (a meal). In Papua New Guinean English you 'have *kaikai*' (a meal). In Tanzanian English you may eat 'at *magengi*', simple and sometimes makeshift eating places. In Nigerian English you may 'eat at a *buka*', a small . . . roofed enclosure usually by the road side where cheap food may be bought and eaten).[1] In the Philippines you may buy an ice *buko*, coconut shavings and water frozen with sugar on a stick, from a *sari-sari* store, a mixed-food business or you may go to a *talipapa*, a small market. If you live in the city, on the other hand, you may go to a *palengke*, a big market.

International dress designers have made some items of clothing, particularly for women, well known throughout the world. Women outside the region where the particular garment originally comes from may be familiar with words such as *sari, sarong, cheongsam* and *mumu*, but there are other words such as the East African *chitenge*, a full length cloth wrap, which is used mainly in the region.

In East African English, the word *shamba* expresses a local concept so much more adequately than words such as *farm, farmlet, smallholding*, etc. ever could. Even if the husband goes into town to work or to look for work, his wife will look after the *shamba*, which may provide enough food for her and the children or enable her to pay the children's school fees.

Words for special regional tools and other implements for cultivation and harvesting have become loan words as their shape and purpose may not have been exactly the same as a related English tool, e.g. the large Malay knife, *parang*, and the Kenyan machete-type *panga*, the Philippine *bolo* and the Singapore/Malaysian *changkol*, a hoe-type implement. Even in urbanized Singapore, a mother was overheard to say to her daughter on a bus:

'When we get home, we ask daddy *to changkol* the garden'

Safari, which has come as a loan word into international English, usually means a 'hunting trip' or at least a rather enterprising and adventurous outing. In East African English, the word *safari*, from kiSwahili 'journey', is not nearly as glamorous. Although it is not used for short routine trips, it means simply 'a journey of some distance', maybe a business trip or a holiday. In Nigerian English, you could 'travel in a *danfo*'. These are 'tiny uncomfortable buses whose drivers are notorious for recklessness'.[1]

Loan words are often found in areas of administration and wherever there is the need to express aspects of the social or political life of a community. Original village structures and administration may depend on the retention of local terms, e.g.[2]

in Ghana:	*penin*	elder	and *okyeame* head spokesman
in Nigeria:	*oga*	headman	
in Cameroon:	*fon*	chief	and *nchinda* spokesman of the chief

In Philippine English, the term *barangays*, originally villages where boats (called barangays) landed, is used for 'the smallest political units in the country',[3] e.g.

How many *barangays* are there in your district?

A *kampung* in Malaysian English expresses a different concept from a European *village* and it is more than can be expressed by the more neutral term *small settlement*. It is a closely structured community with a definite community life and feeling of belonging. In Singapore English, it is spelt *kampong* and, because of increased urbanization and highrise living, is fast disappearing. It is often associated with a particular ethnic group, e.g.

She lived in a Malay *kampong*

The temple belongs to a Chinese *kampong*

The word (*h*)*ulu* in Malay refers to the headwaters of a stream, often a rather quiet, underdeveloped rural area. What can express better the frustration of a smart Singapore secretary who had to take a position in a quiet outer suburb of Singapore than:

'Cause this is quite an *ulu area*, y'know
(implying 'I'm stuck here, away from the main business and shopping areas')

Loan words which relate to traditional festivals, religious observances and celebrations are common. They vary according to cultural traditions and religious beliefs. It is interesting that the medicine man appears as a loan word in a number of the New Englishes, e.g. as the *juju* in Africa, the *bomoh* in Malaysia and the *sinseh* in Singapore.

Names for certain trades and occupations have appeared in the New Englishes, e.g. the *yayas* 'nursemaids' in Philippine English:

If you don't like, *yaya* will give you water[4]

In Indian English, the *dhobi* 'laundry man' and the *durzi* 'tailor' are common. However, as Indians have gone to different parts of the world as merchants and tradesmen, the *dhobi* or *dobi* appears in areas as far apart as East and West Africa and Singapore. An educated East African told us that the word was also used in kiSwahili and claimed that it was 'a Swahili word'.

An interesting, and quite unofficial, profession which flourished in parts of Malaysia and led to a loan word in Malaysian English is the *jaga kereta*. Malay *menjaga* is 'to watch', *kereta* is 'car'. The *jaga* 'watchman' used to be a common sight in Singapore and in Malaysian towns, sleeping on a *charpoy*, a type of bed, in front of the door of the building he was guarding. The *jaga kereta* does not guard cars. He is often a young boy who appears from nowhere and 'assists' you into a parking place, extorting a slight fee. You are wise to pay him if you don't want your car scratched in your absence.

When people express their feelings, they usually resort to familiar expressions. In colloquial Philippine English, if you threaten to pinch someone, you may say 'I'll *kurot* you'. In Singapore and Malaysian English you tell someone angrily:

Don't kacho (or kacau) me when I want to work!
(*kacau* is Malay for 'disturb')

or

Don't *kaypoh* my business! (stick your nose into my affairs)
(*kaypoh* is Hokkien for 'busybody')

And for expressing that something is 'terrific, beyond description' you may, in Singapore English use *shiuk*:

I like hot hot curry — very *shiuk*

and in Ghanaian English *gbeye*:

That film was *gbeye* (really beyond description)

As an educated Ghanaian explained to us:

gbeye defines the intensity of whatever you experience. It could be extreme pleasure or extreme fear.

Loan words are often found when a particular type of person is described. It may be the 'common *tao*', the common man, in Philippine English[3] or the *kāne* (male) and *wahine* (female) of Hawaiian English.[5] An interesting collection of loan words are those which people use to describe themselves or other groups. The local person may be a 'child of the land', *kama'aina*, in Hawaiian English (that is someone born in Hawaii) or a 'prince of the land', *bumiputra* in Malaysian English (that is someone who is born in Malaysia and ethnically Malay or, sometimes, a Malaysian aborigine). Sometimes these expressions get abbreviated, e.g. from a Malaysian Chinese

That hospital, got a lot of *bumi* nurses.

The English writer, E.M. Forster, used the term 'Pinko-Greys' (for Europeans) because it was a more suitable description of their skin colour. The New Englishes have added several interesting loan words to the description of the race of 'Caucasians', e.g.

haole	white person	(Hawaiian English)
gwai ló (Cantonese)	devil	(Hong Kong English)
ang mo kui (Hokkien)	red haired devil	(Singapore/Malaysian English)
orang puteh (Malay)	white man	

Orang puteh is often abbreviated to O.P., e.g.

She's going out with an O.P.

Ang mo kui is shortened to *ang mo* and at times has English plural endings, e.g.

A lot of *Ang Mos* going to that supermarket.

We have already mentioned a number of expressions which really consist of more than one item. Sometimes, one of the items is a loan word and the other one from English. Kachru[6] calls these expressions *hybrids* and puts them into two groups. Words in the first group can appear independently, e.g. from Indian English:

janta meals	(*janta*	— the people, the masses)
lathi charge	(*lathi*	— long iron-bound stick or baton used to control a mob, usually by the police)

With words in the second group, one of the items is usually a grammatical form, such as a suffix, which can appear only in certain combinations, e.g. from Indian English:

-wala (vala)	in *police wala* (someone in the police force)
	-vala is used as an agentive suffix in Hindu-Urdu
-hood	in *brahminhood*
-ism	in *goondaism*
	goonda is a hooligan, a rowdy person

We have said that loan words came into the New Englishes from the background languages of the speakers. One must not forget, however, that among the 'background languages' may also be the pidgins and creoles spoken in the region. West African Pidgin English and Krio have had a considerable influence on the New Englishes of West Africa. In Jamaica, Creole words such as *duppy* are widely used among speakers of Jamaican English. A *duppy*, pronounced [dopi], is 'the spirit of the dead believed to be capable of returning to aid or (more often) to harm living beings . . .'.[7] Words from Tok Pisin are used in Papua New Guinean English, e.g.[8]

wantok	companions, compatriots, fellow (people who have the same speech). It is also the name of a local newspaper which is published in Tok Pisin.
kaukau	sweet potatoes.
bilum	a string-bag made from the bark of a tree which is dried and twined into strings.

tambu	the in-laws (they can be the wife's or the husband's people).
singsing	a celebration or a feast.
didiman	an agricultural officer/adviser. He advises the villagers how to grow better crops.
kiap	a patrol officer who goes to the villages and advises them on government policies.

Words from European nations that explored, administered or traded in certain regions have entered some of the New Englishes, e.g. from Portuguese:

almirah	a cupboard or chest of drawers	(Indian English)[9]
peon	office boy	(Singapore and
amah	domestic servant, nursemaid	Malaysian English)

Formerly, a distinction was made between an *amah*, a female Chinese servant, and an *ayah*, an Indian or Malay/Indonesian servant. Nowadays, the term *amah* is a cover term for all. Actually, many *amahs* in Singapore are now either Tamils or Malays. An exception are the *Black and Whites*, a sought-after and often well-paid group of Chinese amahs, now mostly well over sixty years of age. Their name comes from their traditional way of dress, black trousers and white tunic blouses.

Locally coined words and expressions

The English language is extremely vital and dynamic, shedding dated words and expressions that no longer fulfil a communicative task and coining new ones if they are needed. The New Englishes have had, and are having, their share of this creative process. One way of creating a new word is to add something in the form of a prefix or suffix to already existing words or forms. For example, in colloquial Singapore English, the suffix *-o* is used to form new adjectives or nouns, e.g.

stingko (or *sting*)   smelly
The well water is so stingko — so smelly, you know

cheeko (or *cheeky*)   if someone is *cheeko* or a *cheeko peh*
he has a roving eye and likes to go after girls

cracko   a crazy fellow.

The use of the suffix -*y* is common in a number of the New Englishes. In West African English[10] someone can be *bluffy* (fresh complexioned), and in Indian English[11] something can be *spacy* (spacious). An interesting word is the Singapore English and Malaysian English expression *heaty*. Based on Chinese beliefs, it refers to certain foods and drinks which are supposed to make the body hot, e.g. durian, a popular local fruit. The opposite term to *heaty* is *cooling*.

A common form of transport in the Philippines is the *jeepney*, a small bus – originally army jeeps had been converted to buses – and a popular food is the *bananacue* (or *bananaque*), a 'special type of banana on a stick and cooked like barbecued meat'.[3]

Sometimes the need is felt to distinguish between a male and a female in a profession and the use of the female suffix -*ess* is extended, e.g. in Indian English:

teacher – *teacheress*

Mehrotra,[11] when commenting on the frequent use of the word *teacheress* in matrimonial advertisements, gives two reasons for this coinage:

(1)   Indian languages have two different forms of a word on the basis of sex, for example *adhyapak* (male teacher) and *adhyapika* (female teacher)

(2)   Using *teacheress* instead of *woman teacher* or *lady teacher* is economical and implies some saving for the advertiser.

Prefixes such as *in-*, *out-*, *de-* and *en-* are used to coin new words which may express local customs and activities. In Ghanaian English, for example, *outdooring* refers to the celebration that takes place one week after a child is born. The child is brought 'outdoors' to be named and introduced to friends and relatives. Presents of money are given and publicly announced at the outdooring.

The terms *destool* and *enstool* are used in Ghanaian English for deposing or installing a chief, using the stool as 'a symbol of the ruler's office'[12] e.g.

The people described the *enstoolment* of X as illegal

Nana X claimed that since he had been illegally *destooled* by the old regime, and the N.L.C. brought him back to the stool, he would not give it back . . .

New verbs may be coined on the analogy of existing ones. Often they suggest the opposite of the verb that is already in existence, e.g. in Indian English[9]

to prepone – *to postpone*

where *prepone* means 'to decide to do something earlier than expected'. Word pairs like this can also be created by leaving off a prefix, often a negative prefix such as *un*-, e.g. in East African English:[13]

kempt – *unkempt*

where *kempt* means 'neat and tidy in appearance'.

The most common way of coining new words is by *compounding*, that is using two words which are commonly used in English and combining them to form a new expression. Some of these coinages are word-for-word translations from the background languages; others are formed independently as a result of language strategies. Below, we shall give small samples of the vast selection of new coinages in the New Englishes:

from West African English:[14]

bush meat   game (as opposed to meat from home-bred animals)
We stopped at Awutu to buy some *bush meat*

chewing stick   a short stick that is chewed at one end into a soft brush and used for tooth cleaning

head-tie   a woman's headdress

motor-park   a bus and taxi station from which travellers may board vehicles to other towns

small room   a euphemism for toilet

from East African English:[13]

dry coffee   coffee without milk and sugar

jumbo sale   jumble sale or (in American English) rummage sale

poor money   money for the poor

tea sieve   tea strainer

from Indian English:[11]

change-room   dressing room

four-twenty   cheat or swindler

free-ship   free studentship

from Sri Lankan English:[15]

basket woman   coarsely behaved woman

rice puller   appetizer eaten with rice

from Philippine English:[16]

bed-spacer   someone who rents a bed in a room or dormitory
I have a vacancy for a *bed-spacer*. You can rent one of the four beds in this room.

brown-out   a short interruption to electricity supply

high hat   someone who puts on airs, a snob

standby   one who is idle and merely standing-by
There's a lot of *standbys* at the corner of the street.

a stateside/   general terms to describe goods from overseas or
    a blue label   Western countries. In the Philippines, the cigarette
    or a *blue*   brand 'Marlborough' has a red seal if it is made
    seal   locally and a blue seal if it comes from the USA.

from Singapore and Malaysian English:

hawker centre   an area set aside for hawker stalls, usually selling food. Some of them are semi-permanent.

Later we can eat at the *hawker centre* at Newton Circus

A hawker is a term used for someone who runs a stall, selling food or other goods. It does not have the British meaning of a door-to-door pedlar.

shop house   a two- or three-storey building with a shop on the ground floor and living accommodation on the upper floors. The shops are usually old style businesses such as small provision shops, workshops of tradesmen, etc.

An interesting coinage is the colloquial Hawaiian English expression *da kine*. It is sometimes glossed as 'this kind of' but its uses and its meanings are many, e.g.[17]

Take *da kine* (broom) and sweep da floor

Q: We goin' have one party. I like you come.
A: Where *da kine* (it) goin' be?

Q: You think Sam in love wid Alice?
A: Man, he *da kine* (crazy) 'bout her!

(and referring to rock-music): Oh, *da rock-kine!* I like!

Grammatical shift

By the term *grammatical shift* we mean that a word has either changed its grammatical class, e.g. it has turned from a verb into a noun, or that it has extended its use and can now be used as a verb *and* a noun. Naturally, grammatical changes are also often meaning changes. In the New Englishes, it is more common that words extend their use and can appear in more than one grammatical class. For example, prepositions such as *under, after*, etc. can become verbs, e.g.

from Sri Lankan English:[15]

> *to under*   means 'to let a person down shabbily and dishonestly, to cut his throat, metaphorically'

from Papua New Guinean English:[8]

> *to be aftering something*   to look for something
>
> *to be aftering somebody*   to follow somebody.

Nouns can become verbs. For example in Singapore English and Malaysian English as well as in Jamaican English:

> *to friend*   to be friends with, to befriend.

In all three New Englishes, the expression may have the additional meaning of a sexual relationship, e.g.
from Jamaican English:[18]

> She said if he wanted *to friend* her he would have to go to her mother and ask her.

Verbs may become nouns, e.g.

from Ghanaian English:[12]

> *steer* a steering wheel
> (as a result) he lost control of the *steer* and the car run into a nearby bush.

Nouns may become adjectives, e.g.
from Singapore English:

> Wah, I damn *panic*, you know

or extend their function as well as their meaning, e.g.
from Singapore English:

> The flowers, real one or *bluff one?*
>   (artificial)

> True lah! I never *bluff* you.
>   (I'm not kidding)

> Big *bluff*, man, he!
>   (He's just a show off)

> She asked me to catch the bouquet because she wants me to be the next one to be married. When I told XX, she said *Bluff one!* She caught 6 times already, still the same!

Adjectives and nouns which have become verbs in the New Englishes may be marked for past tense, e.g.[10]

> My gentleman *naked* himself

> Sorry not to have been *chanced* to write before

In some of the New Englishes, adjectives may become past participles and add -*d*, e.g. in Singapore English:

> They feel more *secured*

> She – very *tensed*

And in an advertisement:

> *Matured* secretary required

Nouns may lose their endings to become verbs, e.g.
from Nigerian English:[19]

to barb   cut hair   (from the noun *barber*)

or verbs may acquire endings to become nouns, e.g.
from Papua New Guinean English:[8]

coacher   a coach   (formed from the verb *to coach*)

Meaning changes

Words can change their meanings in different ways. One way would
involve a complete change, that is the word may lose its old meaning
and take on an entirely different one. This is relatively rare. Usually,
traces of the old meaning remain, even if they are only implied. Sey,[32]
for example, mentions that in Ghanaian English, the expression *Town
Council* refers to the *Sanitary Department*.

The meaning of a word may be restricted, so that only part of the
original meaning is implied whenever it is used. This, too, is relatively
rare as often words take on additional new meanings which they did
not have before. One of Sey's[33] examples of restricted use in Ghanaian
English is *donation* which is restricted to 'gifts of money given to
relations of a deceased person to help them to meet the high cost of
funerals'. In British English, the receiver of the donation is usually a
charity or a public fund, not an individual. The word *donations* in
Ghanaian English has therefore not just restricted its meaning but has
taken on an additional meaning as it now extends to private individuals,
even if they are in special circumstances.

A word could keep its original meaning and add new meanings as,
for example, the verb *to branch* in West African English[20] which has
the added meaning of 'call somewhere on one's way to another place',
e.g.

I'm going to branch at my uncle's house.

Extensive studies are necessary to put words and expressions accurately into the different types of meaning changes that we have discussed. Some meaning changes are very regional, others have spread
over a whole nation, e.g. Nigeria, others again beyond the borders of a
nation so that they can be classed as typical for a wider area, e.g. West
Africa. As with the newly coined words, some of the meaning changes
in the New Englishes have been strongly influenced by the background

languages. Others have come about as the result of language strategies. We shall give here some examples from a number of the New Englishes to show the different changes that have occurred in the meaning of English words. Naturally, some of the words mentioned under a particular country may also be found with the same or similar meanings in neighbouring nations or, at least, in a part of the neighbouring nation, e.g. from West African English:[2]

> *balance*   change
> You did not give me any balance
>
> *bush*   unpolished, rural
> He's a proper bushman

from Nigerian English[14]

> *stranger*   guest
> Take some water to the stranger
>
> *fellow*   any person including a female
> David is going to marry that fellow

The same meaning of *fellow* can be found in Singapore English.

> *travelled*   to be away
> My father has travelled (meaning 'My father is away')
>
> *drop*   get out of a car
> I will drop at the roundabout

A similar use of *drop* appears in Singapore English:

> You can drop here   (meaning 'get out here')

In Nigerian English as well as in Singapore English, you *wash* a film or a photo instead of developing it.

from Ghanaian English:[12]

> *fitter*   a motor mechanic or any person who does odd jobs
>   on motor vehicles
>
> *to bring forth* to have a baby
>
> *serviceable*   (used particularly of humans, occasionally of animals)
>   a person who is willing to serve or an animal which
>   is willing to serve, e.g. a serviceable wife, servant,
>   maid, nanny, dog.

from East African English:[13]

cane   hit (not necessarily with a cane)

impregnated   made pregnant
My sister was impregnated by her supervisor

live   to stay, even if the stay is temporary.

In Singapore English, on the other hand, *stay* is used rather than *live,* even if it is permanent, e.g.

I *stay* with my parents (meaning permanently)

from Sri Lankan English:[15]

junction   any place along a road which has one or more shops

from Philippine English:[16]

chancing   (used as a verb) to deliberately touch a woman and
               to make it look like an accident

He always do *chancing* to me

hypocrite   a snob (similar to *high hat* mentioned earlier).

from Singapore English:

alphabets   letters (of the alphabet)
My name, you write it with three *alphabets* not four

The same meaning can be found in Hawaiian English:[17]

My name begins with the *alphabet* A, so I have to go first in line

deep   educated or formal (variety of a language)
My father, he speaks the *deep* Hokkien

to fire someone   to tell someone off
He fired his servant left and right

Another expression used for 'telling off' is to *hammer*

The boss, he really hammer me properly today

side   in the direction of, in the general area of
My flat is Changi side, you know

to sleep (early/late)   to go to bed (early/late)
The people use to *sleep* quite *early*, y'know

New words and new meanings

Christian   This term is often restricted to Protestant religions. The use of this term sometimes causes 'cross-religious' misunderstandings, even in Singapore itself. The writers attended a seminar talk on 'Religion among Singapore Chinese'. The speaker, a Singaporean, gave statistics for the number of *Christians* in Singapore.

Someone (another Singaporean) objected: Your figures are too low, what about Roman Catholics?
Speaker: But they are not Christians.

This was followed by a roar of protest from the Roman Catholic participants.

Some of the expressions used in the New Englishes either still reflect the colonial usage, e.g.

Boy   a male servant or porter in a hotel

in Indian English[11] or they have changed their meaning from colonial times:

colony   has become 'a residential area or block of flats' in Indian English,[9] e.g. Rajendra Colony, Railway Colony

the army *compound* has become 'an enclosed area around a house or a group of buildings' in a number of the New Englishes

to go outstation in Singapore and Malaysia means one leaves the larger town where one is 'staying' to visit smaller places in the country. The telephone operator may say 'this is an outstation call'.

The colonial use of *bungalow* as a detached house with one *or* two storeys is still common in a number of the New Englishes. In British English, a *bungalow* is a single-storey house. In Australian English, it was used for a wooden weekend shack or a small wooden house in the grounds of a larger residence.

Some expressions which have become outdated in some of the more established varieties of English may still be used in the New Englishes, sometimes with a slight change in meaning. We have already mentioned the rather biblical expression *to bring forth* which is used in Ghanaian English[12] for having a baby. Other expressions in Ghanaian English are, for example:

ragamuffin   used jocularly as an expression of mild disapproval
Don't mind him, he's a ragamuffin

trinkets   jewellery, ornaments of great value
The original meaning was 'trifling ornaments of little value'.

In British and Australian English, children could be *scolded*. Nowadays, the expression is becoming outdated and replaced by such expressions as *tell off*. The word *scold* was not usually used for telling off adults, except in a jocular sense.

In Singapore English, everyone can be *scolded*, e.g.

We use to scol(d) these Tamils
(said by a waitress about some Indian hawkers)

It is also possible to *scold* (curse) someone behind their back:

So he scol(d) me, behind of me 'Stupid girl!'
Never mind, let him scol(d) lah!
(said by a salesgirl about a customer)

We have so far talked in general terms about *extension* of the meaning of a word or *changes* in the meaning of a word. Of course, in reality, variation in the meaning of particular words or expressions between a more established variety of English and a New English is far more complex. Some words which may even appear at first to have 'the same meaning' in two varieties of English, e.g. British English and Nigerian English, such as *wife, dog, rain* may have entirely different shades of meaning for an Englishman than they have for a Nigerian. Naturally, every word may have different shades of meaning for one particular person because of past experiences, pleasant or unpleasant, but we are talking here about those shades of meaning that are based on the social and cultural background of the speakers and that may reflect basic social structures within his or her community or nation.

Adejare and Afolayan[21] discuss several fairly basic words such as *wife, dog, rain, flower, coat, mask, work* and show the variation in their meaning between British English and Nigerian English. The word *dog*, for instance, has a basic meaning which is common to both cultures, namely it is a four-legged domestic animal which may bark (if it isn't a Basenji or Dingo!) but in English it usually has the additional meaning of 'being a pet' whereas for the Yoruba in Southern Nigeria it may be *food* (ondo) or *game chaser* (oyu). Adejare and Afolayan talk about the statement made in a television series by a popular British dog trainer 'You must exercise your dog'. They say that

if the same programme were to be screened on NTA Ibadan, Oyo

State, Nigeria, the majority of the viewers would think that the speaker is sick in the head. It would be argued that anybody who has so much free time as to be exercising dogs should be better employed digging holes and filling them up again. . . . For the British, in general, the dog is more than a pet; it is a companion. Since the society is ultra individualistic, a pet, such as a dog or cat, fulfils the role of human companions. It is thus accorded rights that are normally reserved for human beings. . . . The Yoruba society is more corporate in structure in contrast. Families are larger in scope and size. Thus, no one would really lack companionship. And even if he does he would prefer to seek out his kind rather than make do with an animal. This relative unimportance of animals is implied in the Yoruba proverb: 'Eeyan ko ri bi sun, aja nhan an run.' (When human beings have no place to sleep, a dog cannot be allowed any space to snore).

The different structure and size of the African 'family', too, gives rise to differences in the meanings of rather basic words referring to relations within a family,[22] such as *brother, sister, cousin, uncle, aunt*. The term *family* in an African context may mean

(1)   the basic nuclear family in the Western sense, that is: father, mother and children;
(2)   the polygamous family consisting of a father, his wives and all their children;

or

(3)   the extended family, consisting of a father, his sons, or a group of brothers if the father is dead, their wives, sons and unmarried daughters.

Terms such as *father, uncle, brother* and their female equivalents may also be used for people with whom the speaker or writer has no family relationship but for whom he or she feels respect or affection. They also imply ethnic identity. When two people from the same ethnic community and age group meet, for instance, in Lagos or abroad, they may refer to each other as *brother* or *sister*.

What we have said here about Africa, and in particular about Nigeria, is valid, of course, for other New Nations where similar social structures exist.

Idioms

One of the hardest tasks for a non-native speaker of any language is to 'acquire a control' of the idioms of a language, that is to be aware of their exact structure, their meaning and to know when and where to use them. An *idiom* in a language is usually a phrase which has a distinct meaning. This meaning cannot be explained from the separate meanings of the different words in the phrase, e.g. The British English idiom

kick the bucket   to die

In the New Englishes, some interesting new idioms have developed. However, one must realize that there is a whole range of constructions in the New Englishes. There are the learners' attempts to use a British English or American English idiom without being quite successful. These are interesting in themselves as they show up the use of certain language strategies, but they cannot be considered as true, stabilized idioms in the New English.

In some cases it is possible to observe 'an idiom in the making'. In Papua New Guinean English,[8] for instance, there appears to be a tendency to assimilate two idiomatic expressions into one new idiom, e.g.

to be two-minded	to be in two minds
	to be open-minded
to pass the hard times	to have a hard time
	to pass the time
My weight was like dead log	I slept like a log
	to be a dead weight

In Sri Lankan English;[15] there is a tendency to use *put* to form a number of expressions, some of which could be classed as idioms, e.g.

to put a clout	to give someone a clout
Wije *put* the queue breaker *a clout*	
to put a telephone call	to make a telephone call
to put a feed	to have a good meal
to put a catch to	to chase after or woo a member of the opposite sex

Sometimes an idiom from British English may be varied more or less regularly in speech or even in writing because of the different pronunciation in that particular New English (see Chapter 3), e.g. from Singapore English:

the gift of the *gap*

I like to keep my kitchen spick and *spang/spank*

in *lips/leaps* and *bounce*

The last idiom shows the tendency in Singapore English to shorten the [i] sound in such words as *leap*, to reduce a group of three consonants at the end of words to two and to use [s] instead of [z] after a voiced consonant, e.g. *boun(d)s*.

Quite a number of idioms which are widely used by the speakers of the New Englishes are word for word translations from the background languages. For example, the idiom

to shake legs

used in Singapore English and Malaysian English is a translation of the Malay idiom *goyang kaki*. *To shake legs* means 'to be idle', e.g.

Look at you! *Shaking legs* and having a good time.

Stop *shaking legs* and do some work for a change.[23]

In British English, *shake a leg* (in the singular) used to mean 'dance'. Now it has the meaning of 'hurry up'.

Idioms in the New Englishes may be based on certain logical arguments. For example, the idiomatic expression

to declare surplus

used in Nigerian English means 'to host a party'. Jibril[1] comments

. . . presumably because only those who have the money to waste can host parties.

It is often difficult to make a clear-cut division between *idioms* and what we have already discussed as *newly coined words*. Some people use the term *idiom* more widely than others and would include under idioms such expressions as

a been-to   a person who has travelled overseas — usually to Britain which is used in West African English.[20] However, as this expression is an abbreviation of a phrase like 'He/she has *been to* X' and as in this wider context its meaning is quite apparent, it could also be considered as a newly coined expression.

In the following examples of idioms from some of the New Englishes, we have chosen expressions which seem to be genuinely 'idiomatic', e.g.

from East African English:[13]

To be on tarmac to be in the process of finding a new job

from Nigerian English:[14]

To put sand in someone's gari to threaten someone's livelihood or to interfere with someone's good fortune

gari is cassava flour used as a staple food in Southern Nigeria

off head from memory
I can't tell you the number off head

to eat one's cake and have it (British English: to have one's cake and eat it) meaning: it try to enjoy or get advantage from two things; using or doing one of them makes the other impossible, e.g. spending all your money on clothes and wanting it also for going to the cinema.

This usage is also common in Singapore English, e.g.

Decide quickly! You can'(t) *eat your cake and have it*.

From Caribbean English:[24]
Many idiomatic expressions used in Caribbean English are expressions from Caribbean Creole, e.g.

hard ears persistently disobedient or stubborn

cut your eye make a contemptuous gesture with the eyes.

A number of these idioms have their equivalents in idioms found in West African languages.

from Singapore English:

not to have the heart to buy to have no real intention of buying
That customer don'(t) have the heart to buy it – jus(t) bargain bargain for fun

to be in hot soup   to be in trouble

e.g. from a glossary of army slang:[25]

When a soldier is 'screwed upside down' it means that he is
reprimanded very severely and could possibly *be in very hot soup*

In British English, the equivalent idiom would be 'to be in hot water' or
'to be in the soup'

and in very colloquial usage:[26]

to eat snake   to shirk duty
(from Hokkien chiah chôa)

catch no ball   I don't understand, I don't know
from Hokkien   what you are getting at
  liah bô kîu

Groups of verbs

When changes in meaning occur in one word in a language, they usually
affect the meanings of words which are closely related to it. We may
think of words as belonging to a complex network that covers all the
meaning we wish to express in a language. If one word extends its
meaning, a neighbouring word or words in the network may restrict
their meaning or drop out altogether. The way this process works
can be seen in the New Englishes if we look at small groups of related
verbs.

In African English,[27] the meaning of the verb *hear* is extended to
take over some or most of the meanings of *understand, smell* and even
in some cases *feel*, e.g.

I can hear the toilet smelling

I can hear (feel) something on my back

I can hear (understand) five different languages

This reflects the influence of a number of the background languages in
East and West Africa, e.g. Bini, Efik, Hausa, Luo and Swahili.

The extension of meaning for *hear* can also be seen in Singapore
English. Here it has taken on aspects of *understand* and *listen to*:

I can't speak Cantonese — I can *hear* lah!
(meaning: I can understand it)

I like to *hear* Chinese classical music — very nice.

This reflects the influence of the Chinese dialects, e.g. Hokkien.

Some of the background languages to the New Englishes make no distinction between the concepts of *borrow* and *lend*. This is reflected in some of the New Englishes, e.g. in Nigerian English:[27]

Borrow (lend) me your pen

In some New Englishes, the use of *borrow* or *lend* is extended to cover aspects of the meaning of *use*, e.g.

from Hawaiian English:[17]

May I *borrow* your telephone?

and from Singapore English:

Can you *lend* me your sewing machine?
(meaning: May I use your sewing machine?)

In communication between speakers of different varieties of English these utterances may sometimes cause concern for the person asked if she does not want her phone or sewing machine carted out of the house.

Shut the door and *open the light*!

said an East African mother to her child. The use of *open* and *close* for electric switches is common in many of the New Englishes, e.g. East African English, Hawaiian English, Hong Kong English, Malaysian English, Philippine English and Singapore English. It is possible to *open* or *close* lights, fans, radios and the TV. In many cases, a connection can be seen between the extended use of *open* and *close* in a New English and a similar use in the background languages, e.g.

Philippine English	*Tagalog*		
open the radio	buksan	mo	ang	radyo
	open	you	the	radio
close the light	isara	mo	ang	ilaw
	close	you	the	light

Any activity which involves movement, e.g. *go, come, send, carry,*

New words and new meanings

follow, usually involves other concepts as well. We express or imply whether a movement is away from or towards the speaker or writer, whether the person addressed or the person talked about is at the same place as the speaker or not and if the speaker accompanies the person or thing that moves or is moved or whether he or she stays at the same place. In British English many of these concepts are implied by the verb itself, e.g. A says to B:

Come here!	(B moves towards A)
Go there!	(B moves away from A)
Bring me the book!	(B moves with the book towards A)
Take the book over there!	(B moves with the book away from A)

In some languages, some of these directional concepts have to be expressed by additional words, often directional verbs or adverbs. In Tagalog, for example, *punta* means 'come' or 'go', *dalhin* means 'bring' or 'take' and words like *dito* (to this place, here) or *doon* (to that place, there) are used to show in which direction the movement is taking place:

Punta ka dito!	*Punta ka doon!*
come you here	go you there

Dalhin mo ang libro dito!
Bring you the book here

Dalhin mo ang libro doon!
Take you the book there

This is reflected in Philippine English in such orders as:

Go here!   and   *Bring there!*

The Hokkien verbs *gia, théh* and *tòa* can be used for the actions of bringing *and* taking. The same is the case for the Mandarin verbs *ná* and *dài*. The only way one can express in which direction the movement takes place in relation to the speaker is by the addition of directional verbs, such as *khì* (Hokkien) and *qù* (Mandarin) for an action away from the speaker and *lâi* (Hokkien) and *lái* (Mandarin) for an action towards the speaker, e.g.

ná qu	Take it away!
(literally	Bring/take go ———→)
ná lai	Bring it here!
(literally	Bring/take come ←——)

Sometimes these structures are still evident in colloquial Singapore English,[28] e.g.

That book on the TV, *take come here*, can or not?
(Father and son are sitting on the sofa and the latter is sent to fetch a book)

Give him *bring go* lah!
(A nurse is speaking to the clerk who is to give the file to the office messenger, who is to take it to the doctor)

Often, however, the verbs *bring* and *take* are used in Singapore English[28] without additional verbs to indicate direction. The verb *bring* may indicate a movement *away* from the speaker, e.g.

(a clerk speaking to his colleague at the office):
I'm *bringing* these files home

(a teacher to a student who is standing next to him):
Can you *bring* these books to the other table

The verb *take* in Singapore English may have the meaning of *get* or *fetch*.

(Office girl impatiently):
OK, OK I *take* for you, I *take* for you
(meaning: I'll get them for you in a minute!)

In Ghanaian English,[12] the verb *send* may take over the functions of *take away*, e.g.

The children were not to *send* books outside the classroom

In Singapore English, *send* has taken on the additional meaning of 'driving or walking someone to their destination', e.g.

(Host to guest at a party):
Don't worry, I'll *send* you home
(meaning: I'll take you home in my car)

Come, I'll *send* you to the airport
(meaning: I'll give you a lift *or* We'll go together in a taxi)

It's very dark now. We'll *send* you to the main road
(meaning: We'll accompany you, on foot or by car)

and *follow* has the additional meaning of 'go with, come with, accompany', e.g.

I *follow* him to work

We *follow* the coach, you see. They bring us where, we *follow*.
(meaning: We were on a coach tour, you see. Wherever they took
us, we went)

Repetition

A common feature in many of the New Englishes, particular in colloquial speech, is to repeat the same word several times, often to create
a feeling of intensity, e.g.

from Indian English:[6]

hot, hot coffee

long, long hair

from Sri Lankan English:[6]

to go crying, crying

small small pieces

from African English:

We have many many such words

It's really really beyond description

The old old ancestors. . .

The words which are repeated may be nouns, verbs, adjectives or
adverbs. For example, from Jamaican English:[29]

mud-mud	—	a lot of mud
beg-beg	—	repeated acts of begging
preachy-preachy	—	preaching too much

from Malaysian English:

Have you ever taken honeycomb honey — that type of honey,
the *beehive beehive* type?

You watch TV until *late late* — no wonder cannot get up!

from Singapore English:

I don't like this sort of dress — all *frill frill, gather gather*

My son's results terrible, man! All *F F F* — every subject also fail

At one time I like pork very much, you know — morning pork, afternoon also pork, every meal *pork pork pork pork*.

I *find find find* — don't have!
(meaning: I looked high and low for it but I couldn't find it)

Scrub until *clean clean*

Eat until *full full* — then mummy will take you out.

It would appear that in addition to intensity, repetition such as *FFF* and *beehive beehive* also gives a spread of the attribute mentioned. One can picture the Fs in red ink all over a page of a report book or the numerous holes scattered over the honeycomb. *Find find find* too has a visual impact in that it brings to mind the numerous attempts of the person looking for something in various places.

In conclusion, an interesting example of repetition is this comment by a Singaporean on Australians:

Dis Australians, you see dem hold hand hold hand, honey here, honey there, darling here, darling dere, next moment separated already!

CHAPTER 7

New ways of saying it

In the previous chapter, we have looked at the meaning of words and phrases. Naturally, words and phrases do not usually occur in isolation but as parts of larger units. In this chapter we shall look at the ways in which the speakers of the New Englishes structure their sentences, e.g. how word order is used for emphasis, how comparisons are made and how questions may be formed. In fact, as some of our examples in the earlier chapters have been in sentence form, some of the differences in sentence structure between the New Englishes and the more established Englishes will already have been noticed.

Subject and object

No fully satisfactory definition of the two grammatical terms *subject* and *object* has yet been given. This is no wonder as the two terms are difficult to define. Their function in a sentence differs and so does their relationship to the verb, e.g. in

Amy hit Tom

Amy is the *subject* and Tom the *object*. But not all sentences can be analysed as easily as that. It is not really satisfactory to say that the subject is the *doer of an action* as sometimes the verb does not express an action at all, e.g. in

Tom admired Mary

Tom, the *subject* of the sentence, isn't doing anything. He simply has a certain mental attitude towards Mary.

Some books on grammar state that a sentence *must* always have a subject. This, of course, is not true. In English, we have sentences like:

Come here please
Do sit down
Get out!

where there is no subject at all although the person spoken to (or shouted at) can be considered as the subject. It could be said therefore that the pronoun *you* is implied, e.g. (You) come here please.

In more colloquial speech in the 'older' varieties of English, the subject may often be implied rather than overtly stated, e.g.

Q: D'you want to go there this evening?
A: Don't particularly want to.

           or

D'you see much of Bill these days? Never comes round here any more

It is quite obvious that the implied pronoun is *he* and that it refers to Bill.

In the New Englishes, there is a tendency, particularly in colloquial speech, to imply the subject or the object pronoun of a sentence rather than state it explicitly. The meaning is usually quite clear from the context, e.g.

Q: Have you got some friends there?
A: (educated speaker of Indian English) Yes, have got.

The most common object pronoun which is implied, rather than stated, is *it*. This occurs whether the *it* is at the end of a sentence or not, e.g.

from African English:[1]

I'll give (it) to you

from Papua New Guinean English:[2]

Could I ask you people to send (it) to me?

There was a new law but teachers did not follow (it)

from Sri Lankan English:

For example, back home the currency notes – if it is torn, people are reluctant to accept (it)

from Singapore English:

I am very interested in English. That why I must speak (it)

and a common reply in Singapore shops:

Sorry, don't have

Another object pronoun which is treated in this way is *them*, e.g. from Sri Lankan English:

They have the mother-in-law to look after (them)

This statement might have caused some misunderstanding if it had been said in isolation but it was abundantly clear from the context: a discussion of who looked after the children.

When *it* appears as a subject before *is*, it is often implied rather than stated. The following examples are from the colloquial speech of educated speakers of the New Englishes:

Here is not allowed to stop the car	(Hong Kong)
Is very nice food	(Uganda)
No, is not the same	(Nigeria)
But when I move into the flat, is OK	(Philippines)
Is not very interesting, this programme	(Malaysia)

One could argue, of course, that in these examples the *it* is not 'missing' but that it is a matter of pronunciation. *It's* may be reduced to *is* because groups of two final consonants are sometimes reduced to one, e.g. *pits* → *pit*. As many final consonants are often pronounced as voiceless consonants in a number of the New Englishes there is no clue to whether or not this structure is due to phonetic influence.

We feel that often it is not a matter of pronunciation and reduction of a consonant group but rather that the *it* is implied and the *is* is pronounced. There are two main reasons:

(1) This structure occurs in the speech of people who do not frequently reduce groups of two consonants to one.
(2) Constructions like these are quite common in some of the background languages, e.g. in Hokkien

$$Sī\ chin\ phi^n$$
Is very cheap

or simply $Chin\ phi^n$

This is reflected in Singapore English:

Is very cheap, this dress

In certain constructions, *it's* is implied and not stated, e.g.

That means (it's) very competitive, y'know
                        (speaker from Hong Kong)

In my society, (it's) very difficult to have a torn currency note
and then use it
                        (speaker from Sri Lanka)

Each other/themselves

The more established varieties of English make use of two types of pronouns to distinguish between sentences such as:

(1)   The two boys hurt *themselves*   (Reflexive pronouns)
(2)   The two boys hurt *each other*   (Reciprocal pronouns)

Some of the New Englishes, particularly in very colloquial speech, use *ourselves, themselves* for both (1) and (2), e.g.

from African English:[1]

They love themselves

They speak to themselves in English

This reflects some of the African languages which do not make a distinction between the two types of pronouns.

Focussing and emphasizing

A very common feature in many of the New Englishes is what is sometimes called *pronoun copying*. This is the practice of adding a pronoun after the noun subject of a sentence, e.g.

My *mother she* works very hard

This occurs in the 'older' Englishes as well but here it is confined, strangely enough, to a rather pompous oratorical style or a very colloquial style, e.g.

(from a political speech):
. . . and those *trouble makers, they* should be dealt with in no uncertain terms!

(overheard in the supermarket)
My mum she's ever such a good cook

In the New Englishes, it is used quite extensively and more frequently than in the more established varieties, e.g.

from East African English:[3]

My daughter she is attending the University of Nairobi

from Hong Kong English:

Our Chinese people we like fish very much the shrim(p)s

from Bangladesh English:

People they don't have that sort of belief now

from Jamaican English:

The black Americans they speak English

from Fijian English:

Most Indians they know Fijian

from Singapore English:

But *the grandson(s) they* know to speak Malay

Of course, it is a perfectly legitimate device for emphasizing the subject, which is quite commonly used in educated varieties of other languages, e.g. in French

Ma mère, elle est très élégante

It is a particularly useful device for speakers of the New Englishes who do not make the same use of intonation for emphasizing as do some of the speakers of British English (see chapter 8).

Actually it is not only the subject of a sentence which may be treated in this way. If the object occurs at the beginning of the sentence, it may also be 'copied' by a pronoun which occurs later in the sentence, e.g.

from Sri Lankan English:[4]

Kasy, I expect *him* to make an exciting contribution to Tamil studies

from Papua New Guinean English:[2]

Some teachers when I was in high school I liked *them* very much

Another method of emphasizing a word or group of words, which is common in some of the New Englishes, is simply to put it to the beginning of the sentence, e.g.

from an educated speaker of Indian English:

Because *Hindi* they have declared as National Language

In Singapore English, for example, this method of *focussing* can be used for the object of a sentence, whether it is a direct object or an indirect object, e.g.

Certain medicine we don' (t) stock in our dispensary

One subject they pay for seven dollar(s)

To my sister sometime I speak English

Comparison

If an adjective does not have a special comparative form, e.g. *better, friendlier, nicer*, the usual comparative construction in the more established varieties of English is

X is more _____ than Y

e.g. Jill is more intelligent than her sister. In some of the New Englishes the word *more* in these constructions is sometimes omitted, e.g.

from West African English:[3]

It is the youths who are skilful in performing than the adults from Papua New Guinean English:[2]

He was clever than the rest

from Sri Lankan English:

The unemployment position is much severe than Singapore

Sometimes *more* is not used in constructions such as

X likes A more than B

e.g. from African English:[1]

He values his car than his wife

The reason for this may be the fact that the comparative is often expressed with just a single word in African languages.

Word order

Often, in the New Englishes, words or groups of words occur in a different order from what is usual in the 'older' Englishes. This word order may reflect the word order in the background languages. Gonzalez[5] mentions cases of Tagalog influence on Philippine English, e.g.

'I have seen you *already*' as against 'I have already seen you'

'He did not come *unfortunately*' as against 'Unfortunately he did not come'

Similar 'movement' of adverbs occurs in the following examples of spoken English. The position which the adverb or adverbial group would have had in the more established varieties of English is indicated by ( ). It can be seen that, in each case, words such as *already, only*, etc. are put *after* the word or word group that the speaker wishes to emphasize:

By the time I graduate I will ( ) be too old *already*
(speaker from Hong Kong)

We used to talk ( ) in Hindi *only*
(speaker from India)

Some parents do not ( ) accept Western education *even*
(speaker from Papua New Guinea)

Too/also/either and already/yet

Speakers of the New Englishes prefer the use of *also* to *too*. *Also* may appear in sentence final position, e.g.

from Malaysian English and Singapore English:

This is quite nice *also*

Have Chinese people, English, Malay *also*

But we are supposed to take Chinese (Mandarin) *also*

An interesting feature of English is the positive-negative alternation between *too/also* and *either* and between *already* and *yet*:

POSITIVE: I'm going and George is going *too*
NEGATIVE: I'm not going and George isn't going *either*
POSITIVE: Eliza went to the supermarket and *also* to the post office
NEGATIVE: Eliza didn't go to the supermarket or to the post office *either*
POSITIVE: You've *already* finished?
NEGATIVE: You haven't finished *yet*?

With some speakers of the New Englishes, there is no alternation. Only the positive word is used in positive *and* negative sentences, e.g.

from Philippine English:[5]

He hasn't seen Maria *also*

from Hawaiian English:[6]

I called you up but you weren't there *already*
(meaning: . . .you weren't there *yet*)

In Singapore English, both *yet* and *already* are used but somewhat differently. The above Hawaiian English example would mean to many Singaporeans:

I called you up but you had left

To express the meaning implied by the Hawaiian English example, a Singaporean may say:

I called you up but you diden come yet

Expressions of time

It is common in Malaysian English and Singapore English to use *before* and *after* as adverbs. Two other expressions that are frequently used are *last time* and *wait*.

Before and *last time* often have the meaning of 'formerly', 'previously' or 'in the past'.

For example, a shopkeeper might say:

> *Before* sell at dis price can, now cannot already, because everyting so expensive, y'know

Someone living in a highrise flat might say:

> *Last time* I lived in kampong, y'know

Last time reflects the Chinese expression:

téng pái	(Hokkien)	previous time, last time
shàng cì	(Mandarin)	

The adverbs *wait* and *after*, a contracted form of *afterwards* which may also be used, have a number of meanings. In example (1) *after* (*wards*) implies 'afterwards' *and* 'or else', in example (2) *wait* means 'later', which can be several hours later, and in example (3) *wait* implies 'later/afterwards' *and* 'or else':

(1)   Don't do that *after* (or *afterwards*) you get caning then you know

(2)   *Wait* I return the book to you

(3)   Better book now, *wait* got no more seats on the plane

The use of *wait* shows the influence of expressions in the background languages such as *tan* in local colloquial Hokkien and *nanti* in Bazaar Malay and Baba Malay.

Connecting sentences

In a number of New Englishes, conjunctions may be omitted, particularly in colloquial speech. This may occur when sentences of equal status are joined e.g.

from colloquial Singapore English:

So we sit down, wait for my uncle to come

It also occurs frequently in conditional sentences, where *if* is omitted, e.g. from colloquial Singapore English:

You go by meter, you got to pay

(talking about Chinese characters):
Leave only one stroke out, wrong already

(talking about charges at a public swimming pool):
Stay longer, they have to over charge (charge more)

This use reflects the influence of Chinese dialects and Mandarin where conjunctions are not always needed to link sentences.

The use of *suppose, if suppose* or *supposing* can also be found frequently in some of the New Englishes, e.g.

from Indian English:

Suppose I did my Bachelor, I would. . .
(Bachelor of Arts degree)

from Singapore English:

Supposing that a student was to fail in the first year. . .

He said 'We like to go *if suppose* we hear there's a danger. We jus(t) like to go and see. We like to experience it!'

There are many ways in a language of logically connecting one sentence with the sentence before or after it. We shall mention only one interesting new expression that occurs in Malaysian English and Singapore English. Its function is to enumerate and also, in some case, to reinforce. It is similar in meaning to *What's more* or *On top of that*, e.g.

from Singapore English:

Some more he's a very cheeky fella at dat time. He got two wife ah. *Some more* he see pretty girl only, sure chase after

from Malaysian English:

My room no sunlight one, morning also no sunlight, afternoon also no sunlight. *Some more* my room ah, no air one, open window also no wind one

A word which is used very frequently in colloquial Malaysian English and Singapore English is *so*. It has many functions.[7] Some of them are different from those of the more established varieties of English:

(1)   It may be used instead of *then* in sentences such as:
        If the age is under, *so* they stay another year

        If (we) speak of something not the school business, *so* we speak in Chinese or other dialect, you see

(2)   It may take the place of *if*, e.g.
        So you come late, you don'(t) know where to park

(3)   It may replace *that* in clauses such as:
        No, I don't think *so* my English is that good

(4)   It may be used to introduce a sentence. Here it often does not have the meaning of *therefore*. There seems to be no obvious link to the preceding sentence. It appears to have a similar function to the Malay sentence introducer *maka*:

        Q: What language or dialect do you speak to the other students?
        A: *So* it depend lah. If discussing the book we speak English

        Q: When did you learn Mandarin?
        A: *So* when I completed my primary education, *so* I just take some night class of those Mandarin, that's right

Questions

In any language, there are two main types of questions:

(1)   The type of question which is sometimes called in English an *open question* or a *WH-question*. It asks who, what, when, where, why, how, e.g.
        Who's coming to the meeting?
        Why are you leaving so early?

(2)   The type of question which requires a 'yes' or 'no' answer — although, of course, not always a bland 'yes' or 'no' which, in some societies, would be considered abrupt and rude. This type is sometimes called in English the *yes/no* question, e.g.

Are you going to work tomorrow?

Did you remember to post that letter?

We shall not consider here the fact that some questions may function as orders, requests, etc.

In quite a number of the New Englishes, the word order in WH-questions is different. There is, for example, no inversion after the question word. Instead of:

What would you like to eat?
When would you like to come? or

speakers of Indian English[8] may say:

What you would like to eat?
When you would like to come? or

This type of structure is also found in other New Englishes, e.g. from Singapore English and Malaysian English:

Where the children go ah?
Where the children gone ah? or
(meaning: Where have the children gone to?)

As we have mentioned in Chapter 5, it is common in colloquial Singapore English and Malaysian English, as it is in other colloquial varieties of the New Englishes, not to use the verb *do* to form questions

What time he come?

The expressions *what for* or *for what* often replace *why*, e.g.

What for you want to do that?
Wear until so nice, *for what?*

When a WH-question is reported, it is quite common for speakers or writers of some of the New Englishes to use inversion after the question word, e.g.
from Indian English:

I asked Hari where *does he* work[9]

Do you know what *will be the rate*?

In the more established varieties of English, it is common not to invert, e.g.

Do you know what *the rate will be*?

although inversion occasionally takes place in very colloquial speech, e.g.

She asked me where *was I* going to put it

With YES/NO questions there is a tendency in some of the New Englishes to use the same word order as in statements but to show that a question is asked by means of rising intonation at the end, e.g.

You come tomorrow?

Sometimes a short additional word, often called a *question particle*, is added, e.g.

from Papua New Guinean English:

You are going, ah?

from Singapore English:

You don't want, ah?

from Sri Lankan English:[4]

You were able to do it, ah?

Expressions which are added to form YES/NO questions are called *question tags*. Some languages use an invariant question tag, e.g. German *nicht wahr?* (not true?) and French *n'est-ce pas?* (isn't it?). The more established varieties of English have a very complex system of question tags. This often appears as an impenetrable maze to any learner of the language, e.g.

He got married, didn't he?

She wouldn't have said that, would she?

I'll be invited too, won't I?

A negative statement can only be followed by a positive question tag but a positive statement may be followed by a positive or negative question tag depending on context and situation.[10]

The New Englishes usually (and very sensibly) avoid this 'maze of constructions' by using one or two question tags only. The most common ones are *no? not so? is it?* and *isn't it?*

Indian English uses *no? isn't it?* and *is it?*, e.g.

You went there yesterday, isn't it? (no?)

You are coming this evening, isn't it? (no?)[9]

The advertisement will cost you 20 dollars, isn't it?

Is it? is often used in certain polite responses to statements, e.g.

A: The second session will start at 1.30
B: Ah, is it?

A: We start the day by singing the National Anthem
B: Oh, is it?

A similar use of *is it?* can be found in Malaysian English and Singapore English.

In the New Englishes, *isn't it* may be used after negative as well as positive statements, e.g.
from Indian English:[8]

You are going tomorrow, isn't it?

He isn't going there, isn't it?

Kachru[8] suggests the influence of Hindi-Urdu, which uses the invariable particle *na* as a question tag after all statements.

Sri Lankan English[4] uses *no?* and *isn't it?*, e.g.

Upili returned the book, *isn't it?*

West African English frequently uses *isn't it?* or *not so?*,[11] e.g.

He loves you, *isn't it/ not so?*

It doesn't matter, *not so?/ isn't it?*

Todd,[11] when discussing English in Cameroon, suggests that the question tag *not so?* 'is clearly influenced by the expression in Pidgin *no bin so?*, e.g.

He got married, *not so?*
i bin mari,   *no bin so?*

In Singapore English and Malaysian English, both *is it?* and *isn't it?* are used,[12] both with rising intonation, e.g.

You check out now, *is it?*

You want Carlsberg, *isn't it?*

Is it? is often used to obtain confirmation of a fact that has already been mentioned, e.g.

I want it at six o'clock
At six, *is it?*[13]

or confirmation of a fact that has been implied. For example when a certain extension was requested, the operator at the firm's switchboard replied:

You want Mary, *is it?*

It was, in fact, Mary's extension which had been requested. Sometimes, *is it* is used as a tag for a straightforward question where the answer may be *yes* or *no*, as in:

Your husband also read Jawi, *is it?*

It also occurs after negative statements:

You are not going home, *is it?*

The case of *isn't it* is more complex. One of its uses is as a question tag after positive statements, e.g.

You know my boss, *isn't it?*

One particular type of YES/NO question which is obviously influenced by Chinese structures is found in Singapore English and Malaysian English. This is the 'X or not' type, e.g.

You come tomorrow, can or not?

This chicken, good or not?

All churches use the same, true or not?

In the last example, the speaker would expect the other person to agree.

Summary

To sum up, there are certain tendencies which are common to some or most of the New Englishes:

(1)   a tendency to imply rather than explicitly state subject and object pronouns which can be understood from the context;

(2)   a tendency to use pronoun copying;
(3)   a tendency to use adverbs such as *already, only, even* in
      sentence final position;
(4)   a tendency not to invert in WH-questions and YES/NO
      questions;
(5)   a tendency to use invariant question tags.

CHAPTER 8

New tunes on an old language

We have already mentioned in Chapter 3 that the usual first impression anyone has of a speaker of a New English is that he or she 'sounds different' or 'has a different accent'. In that chapter we discussed some of the differences which can be noticed in the sounds of the language: the vowels and consonants. We also pointed out that varieties of English which have been spoken for a long time, the so-called 'native varieties' also differ in this respect. Some have an *r*-sound in words like *her, cart, work*, while others do not. There are differences in the vowels of words like *chance, after, glass* and many other differences which help us to identify a speaker as coming from the USA, Scotland, the South of England, Australia and so on. Combinations of differences of this kind also help us to identify a speaker of a New English as coming from West Africa, India, Singapore, Jamaica and so on.

However, these are not the only clues which help us to identify the varieties of English, old or new. If all varieties of English were spoken with the same intonation, they would sound far more similar to one another, even though the vowels and consonants differed.

To simplify matters, we shall first consider words in isolation. Of course, words very rarely do occur in isolation except when a list is being read out or when, for example, someone asks for the meaning of a word. However, native speakers of languages like English do generally have the feeling that in words of two or more syllables, one of the syllables stands out. This is commonly referred to as the *stressed syllable* or the *accented syllable* and dictionaries indicate this by various means, e.g. a mark before the syllable:

'cobweb, 'convert (noun), con'vert (verb).

Of course, even the older varieties of English differ as to which syllable takes the primary stress. There are typical differences between American and British English (with Australian English sometimes following the British and sometimes the American pattern). There is also variation from one speaker to another. The following pairs show some of the differences between typical British and American stress patterns (stressed syllables are in italics):

British	American
re*search*	*re*search*
hot *dog*	*hot* dog

(for a type of sausage in a bread roll)

*am*ateur	ama*teur*

Sometimes there is also a difference in spelling as with:

alu*min*ium	*alu*minum
speci*al*ity	*spe*cialty*

*also usual Australian patterns

We have said that native speakers of English feel that a certain syllable is more accented or stressed. Why is this? There are four features which help to give this impression of accent or stress:

1 *loudness*   Usually, the accented syllable is louder than the other syllable or syllables in a word, especially if the word is said in isolation.
2 *length*   The vowel of the accented syllable is often longer than any other vowel or vowels in the word.
3 *quality*   Often the vowels in the unstressed syllables are changed to the 'schwa' [ə], as mentioned in Chapter 3, e.g.

*con*vert ['kɒnvɜ:t] (noun), con*vert* [kən'vɜ:t] (verb)

4 *pitch*   Typically, when a word is said in isolation there is a change in pitch on the accented syllable. This means that on the accented syllable the speaker's voice rises or falls. If we consider the *convert* pair again, it is usual to say the noun in isolation with a fall on *con-*: cònvert and to say the verb in isolation with a rise followed by a fall on *-vert*: convêrt. In connected speech, of course, the pitch movement varies according to other factors which we shall discuss later.

Although some people recognize an accented syllable mainly because of a rise or fall in the speaker's voice, others, including native speakers of English, rely to quite an extent on the other three factors.

In many of the New Englishes, stress patterns may differ considerably from those of the more established varieties of English. For example, in an examination of 210 words of three or more syllables spoken by Singaporeans,[1] it was found that 72 had a different stress pattern. In 69 cases, the syllable which sounded more stressed occurred *later* in the word than the syllable which would have been stressed in Southern British English, e.g.

Singapore speakers	*Southern British English*
edu*ca*ted	*ed*ucated
prefer*ence*	*pref*erence
criti*cism*	*crit*icism
distri*bu*ted	dis*trib*uted
usual*ly*	*u*sually

In some of these words, the syllable appeared to be stressed because of length, e.g. the common Singaporean pronunciation of *usually* has a longer final vowel than in Southern British English, that is [iː] rather than [i] or [ɪ].

Often the vowel quality is different too. For example, in the Singaporean pronunciation of *preference*, the vowel in the last syllable is usually the open *e*-sound [ɛ] sometimes pronounced with length [ɛː], whereas in Southern British English it is the very short centralized *e*-sound [ə].

In all cases, the pitch movement was different. The Singaporean speakers uttered the italicized syllables on a higher pitch. This differed from the typical pitch movement in Southern British English and, in general, from other more established varieties of English.

It has been claimed that because in Panjabi there is a strong tendency to accent the second syllable of a word, Panjabi Indians tend to do the same when speaking English.[2] On the other hand, Indians from Rajasthan are said to have a 'strong tendency . . . to place the accent on the first syllable of words'. This is also said to be the case for native speakers of the Southern Indian language, Telugu, when speaking English.[3]

In West Africa, there appears to be an influence from the local tonal languages such as Yoruba. A word like *father* would be said with a high-toned syllable followed by a low-toned syllable.[4] Of course, as an isolated word, the first syllable is likely to have a higher pitch when said by speakers of the more established varieties of English, but in conversation it would depend on the type of utterance. For example, it is possible in an utterance like:

When I told my father, he didn't seem very pleased

for the pitch to rise on the *second* syllable of *father*.

In Nigerian Pidgin, some words are distinguished by differences in tone. For example, *fádà* (high tone followed by low tone) is 'father' while *fàdá* (low tone followed by high tone) is a 'Roman Catholic priest'.[5] This type of pitch distinction could have an influence on the local variety of English.

Speech rhythm

In connected speech, different languages have different rhythms. This is due to several factors.

In some languages, the accent is always or nearly always on the same syllable as we saw before in connection with some of the languages of India. In Malay, the accented syllable is nearly always the penultimate (the last but one) whereas in some Aboriginal languages of Australia it is always the first. In other languages, such as English and German, accented syllables may occur anywhere in a word. These differences in word accent can give rise to quite different effects in longer stretches of speech.

There is another factor to be considered. In some languages, the difference between stressed and unstressed syllables is not very great. In others, such as some varieties of English as spoken in England, it is considerable. Many unstressed vowels occur as the short centralized *e*-sound [ə] or disappear altogether. A word like *company*, which in some varieties of English, such as American and Australian, has three syllables, may appear to have only two in Southeastern British English: *compny*.

English has been referred to as having a *stress-timed* speech rhythm.[6] This means that the stressed syllables occur at equal intervals in time. For example,[7] in:

Álison didn't | fínish her | éssay
   1   2   3

each of the three segments (marked 1, 2, 3) would take the same time to utter, although each segment has a different number of syllables. The effect is that the stressed syllables (marked ´) occur at equal intervals.

Stress-timed is a convenient term but it should not be taken too literally. Recorded speech of British English shows that, although English has a tendency to a stress-timed rhythm, it is not strictly stress-timed. However, there is a general impression when listening to some speakers of English that the more prominent syllables occur at fairly regular intervals.

Other languages, such as French, are considered to have a *syllable-timed* speech rhythm.[6] This means that all syllables occur at equal intervals in time. For example,[7] in:

Il / est / ar/ri/vé / á / six / heures
1 2 3 4 5 6 7 8

he (is arrived)   at six o'clock
    arrived

the segments marked 1, 2, 3, etc. would each take the same time to utter. As each segment consists of one syllable, each syllable occurs at equal intervals of time.

Again, recorded speech of French shows that there is a tendency to a syllable-timed rhythm but that not necessarily every syllable takes exactly the same time. When one listens, however, to a speaker of French, one has the overall impression that syllables come regularly one after the other until a longer syllable occurs at the end of a word group.

Syllable-timed rhythm is a characteristic which has been noticed in many of the New Englishes, e.g. West African English,[8] Jamaican English,[9] Hong Kong English,[10] Singapore English,[11] Malaysian English,[11] and some varieties of Hawaiian English.[12] Indian English has been referred to as 'neither syllable-timed nor stress-timed'.[13] Presumably this was said because Indian English is not as strongly stress-timed as some native varieties of English.

Why should so many of the New Englishes tend to be syllable-timed? To a great extent this can be explained by the influence of the background languages, Chinese, which in its various dialect forms is the background language in Hong Kong and one of the background languages in Singapore and Malaysia, is syllable-timed. West African languages such as Yoruba are also syllable-timed and this is a characteristic of Nigerian Pidgin.[5] As we have seen, however, Indian languages do have accented syllables, although typically the position of the accented syllables is more regular than in English. As mentioned before, the difference between stressed and unstressed syllables may be less than in English. It has been claimed that Hindi stress 'is far weaker than in English, perhaps because unstressed syllables are not detectably reduced as they are in English' and 'no words are differentiated solely by stress'.[14]

Differences in speech rhythm can sometimes cause problems in communication between speakers of different varieties of English, even among the more established varieties. Speakers of some varieties of British English are sometimes accused by Americans and Australians of 'gobbling up words' or 'swallowing syllables'. These same speakers, however, may think that Americans and Australians speak with a drawl or sound monotonous.

Speakers of syllable-timed languages, whose variety of New English also tends to be syllable-timed, often feel that the more strongly stress-timed varieties of English are difficult to understand, while the more syllable-timed New Englishes may sound strange and, at first, difficult to understand for the speaker of a more established variety because content words do not seem to 'stand out' sufficiently. We shall take up this matter again when discussing 'contrastive stress'.

Discourse intonation

Utterances in English are made up of *tone groups* (or *tone units*). In each group there will be a change in pitch, either rising or falling, on a particular syllable, called the *tonic syllable*. In a word of two or more syllables, the tonic syllable would always be the *accented* syllable of a word. For example, if in speech there was a change in pitch on the word *converSAtion*, it would occur on the third syllable but not on the first, second, or fourth.

In an utterance like:

When I came HOME I saw FRED

there would be a change in pitch on HOME and on FRED. If the speaker believes that the other person did not know *who* was seen when the speaker came home, there would be a fall in pitch on FRED. This falling tone has been called the *proclaiming tone*[15] because the

137

speaker is 'proclaiming' what he or she thinks to be new information for the other person. On the word HOME there would be a fall and then a rise in the speaker's voice. This fall-rise tone has been called the *referring tone*[15] because the speaker is not providing new information but is referring to what he or she believes to be 'known' to the other person. The word 'known' here can mean 'previously referred to' or 'generally understood as usual'. In this case, it is understood that the speaker would 'come home'.

On the other hand, the speaker could have used a proclaiming tone on HOME and a referring tone on FRED:

When I came HOME/ / I saw FRED

This would have been an appropriate answer to:

When exactly did you see Fred?

Of course, frequently the 'known' is mentioned before the 'unknown'. Therefore the answer could quite likely have been

I saw FRED/ / when I came HOME

In this example, the pitch movement for the proclaiming tone and the referring tone is on the last syllable of each tone group. (We have marked the end of a tone group by / /.) However, the syllable on which the pitch movement begins, the tonic syllable, may not be the last syllable in the tone group, e.g.

When you see MAry this afternoon // ask her to CALL on me
referring tone   proclaiming tone

When someone reads aloud, e.g. reading a passage from a book, a message or an item of news, a *zero tone* may be used instead of the referring tone. This occurs when the reader concentrates more on simply saying 'what is printed on the page' and is not concerned with interacting with the hearer. When the zero tone is used, the pitch of the voice rises only slightly at the end of the tone group.

In addition to the tonic syllable, other syllables occurring before it in a tone group may be given prominence by combinations of the features we have mentioned before: length, loudness, quality and pitch movement. However, the pitch movement on them will not be as noticeable as the movement which starts on the tonic syllable. We shall indicate prominent syllables by CAPITAL LETTERS and the tonic syllables by CAPITAL LETTERS and underlining.

In a sentence like:

PerHAPs he'll come toMORrow

the speaker may give prominence to *perhaps* and *tomorrow* but the fall in pitch which marks the proclaiming tone will start with the second syllable of *tomorrow*. This is so because *tomorrow* is the new information. However, *perhaps* is also given prominence as it reflects the speaker's attitude towards the information he is supplying, namely that he isn't quite sure about it.

In reading a passage of text, native speakers may give different interpretations. They may give prominence to different words and may vary in their choice of tone. However, native speakers of the more established varieties of English are unlikely to make certain choices. Speakers of some of the New Englishes, however, *do* have different intonation systems. To the speaker of a more established variety, they appear to give prominence to words which speakers of the more established varieties would not expect to be made prominent. They also have differences in tone, using, for example, what seems like a proclaiming tone with a falling pitch when a referring tone might be expected. In addition, the pitch movement may start on a different word or syllable than would be likely in, for example, Southern British English.

The following examples, read from the same text, show differences between a speaker with an RP[16] accent and three educated speakers of New Englishes.[17] Some slight changes in word order have been made by the speakers as they were reading the text. Divisions between tone units are shown by //. Whenever the speaker used a *referring tone*, the tone unit has been marked by *r*, when he used a proclaiming tone, it has been marked by *p*. A zero tone is shown by *o*.

RP speaker

r Where two groups of speakers develop closer social contacts than they PREviously HAD // *o* their language is quite likely to conVERGE.// *p* This apPEARS to have happened in JaMAIca // *r* where the language spoken toDAY is much more like BRITish English // *p* than it was two hundred YEARS ago.//

Jamaican speaker

p Where two groups of speakers develop closer social conTACTS // *r* is than they had previous<u>LY</u> // *o* their language is quite LIKEly // *p* to con<u>VERGE</u>. // *r* This appears to have happened in JaMAIca // *p* where the language spoken to<u>DAY</u> // *o* is much more like British English // *p* than it was two hundred years a<u>GO</u>.//

West African speaker

o Where two groups of speakers develop // *p* closer social <u>CON</u>tacts // *o* than they <u>HAD</u> // *o* previously // *p* their language is quite likely to con<u>VERGE</u>. // *r* This appears to have happened in JaMAIca // *p* where the language spoken to<u>DAY</u> // *p* is much more like British ENGlish // *p* than it was two hundred years a<u>GO</u>.//

Indian speaker

r Where two groups of speakers develop CLOSer social <u>CON</u>tacts // *r* than they <u>HAD</u> previously // *p* their language is quite likely to con<u>VERGE</u>. // *r* This apPEARS to have happened in JaMAIca // *r* <u>WHERE</u> // *p* the language spoken toDAY is much more like <u>BRIT</u>ish English // *r* than it <u>WAS</u> // *p* two hundred <u>YEARS</u> ago.//

It must be emphasized that these differences in intonation are not to be considered as *wrong*. They may reflect intonation patterns in the background languages, but if they are widely used among a group of New English speakers then they are simply characteristic of that New English. Of course, sometimes prominence is given to a syllable different from what would be expected in the hearer's own variety of English. This may sound unusual but it is only occasionally that misunderstanding will occur, especially if there is mutual tolerance. The following are some examples from recorded interviews with educated speakers of New Englishes:

> *p* If Yoruba speakers are having a conversation I wouldn't understand what they are talking a<u>BOUT</u> (Nigerian speaker)
> (instead of TALKing about)

> *p* They can't afford to go to secondary <u>SCHOOL</u> (Kenyan speaker)
> (instead of SECondary school)

> *r* So I was new <u>HERE</u> // *p* I don't know where to <u>GO</u> (Philippine speaker)
> (instead of NEW here)

p She told me I have no retention <u>POWER</u> (Hong Kong speaker) (instead of reTENTion power)

p you will avoid speaking your own (language) and LEARN the main <u>ONES</u> (Zambian speaker)

Instead of *r* You will avoid speaking your OWN language // *p* and LEARN the <u>MAIN</u> ones

At times, it is possible that a difference in intonation can make the listener feel that *contrastive stress* is being used. In English, contrastive stress involves a move to a higher pitch. For example someone may say:

That was Tom's <u>WIFE</u>

in answer to the question:

Was that Tom's sister?

An utterance by a Singaporean like:

p I talk to ^{HER} Canton<u>ESE</u>

may be understood as emphasizing *her* rather than someone else. However, in Colloquial Singapore English, other devices are used instead of contrastive stress, such as putting the item to be contrasted to the beginning of the sentence:

This kind cannot get already
(You can't get *this* kind any more)

or a discourse particle may be used.

Discourse particles

In the more established varieties of English, intonation can be used for emphasis or to express the attitude of the speaker to the other person, the situation or the topic. There is no absolute one-to-one relationship between intonation and the speaker's attitude. It depends on the situation and what is said. What may sound 'lively and cheerful' in one situation may sound 'abrupt and rude' in another. However, some intonation patterns do seem to go with certain attitudes, e.g.

We <u>WON</u> (with a rise and sharp fall on *won*)

could express surprise and:

Take CARE of yourSELF (with CARE starting on a higher pitch
than 'take' and then falling and with a slight fall followed by a
rise on SELF)

could express the speaker's concern.

Some languages, however, do not make use of intonation on the content words in this way but make extensive use of *discourse particles*,
usually one syllable words which have no separate meaning as such but
whose function is to convey the attitude of the speaker. Some of these
particles are carried over into informal speech in a number of the New
Englishes.

For example, in the speech of the *yayas*, Philippine nursemaids, the
clause final particle *ha* is said to express 'importunity'.[18] The following
examples seem to be seeking the child's agreement:

Don't do that again *ha* because Jesus will get mad at you if you
do that again

I'll give you na lang something *ha*?

The expression *na lang* is said to mean 'just' or 'only'.

Colloquial Singapore English makes extensive use of particles from
the Southern Chinese dialects. Some of these particles have different
functions according to differences in tone and length, depending on
the mood and attitude of the speaker:

Persuasion	*lah* with a fall in pitch Come with us lah!
Annoyance	*lah* with a rise in pitch Wrong lah! Tsch! Write again here!
Strong objection	*lah* with a sharper fall in pitch A: Shall we discuss this now? B: No lah! So late already
Displeasure	*ah* with a sharp rise in pitch Never listen ah!
Surprise	*ah* with a slight fall in pitch He won ah! (He won, did he?)
Yes/No questions	*ah* with a fall in pitch This belongs to him ah?

WH questions and alternative questions   *ah* with a rise in pitch

Where is Gordon ah?

Can we make it or not ah?

Soliciting agreement   what or *ma* with a fall in pitch

Here, the English 'what' often replaces the Chinese particle. It is possibly a transfer from the archaic English usage as in:

Damned impertinent what!

Jolly decent what!

Examples from Singapore English include:

A: Have you been to the H (restaurant)?
B: Yes, the food there not bad what — can try lah

Commenting at the end of a show:

Not bad what, the show?

This particle may also be used to express disagreement or disapproval:

A: This Chinese silk blouse very expensive ah?
B: Not nice what

A: Where have you been S?
B: I go rounding what
   (I've been running errands) B is defensive and annoyed.

A: Your little girl is very naughty
B: My mother in law what. Spoil her like nobody's business

An example with a *ma* particle showing disagreement is given below:

A: That machine very hard to operate — so many buttons!
B: Easy ma! Come I show you

For Singaporean speakers of English, dialogue without these particles would seem over-formal. The particles perform functions which are performed by intonation alone in some other varieties of English.

We have been able to deal with only some of the ways in which the New Englishes have modified the intonation patterns of the older varieties. However, it will be obvious that just as the New Englishes have produced their own distinctive types of pronunciation, new grammatical structures, new words and new meanings for old ones, so they have produced new and distinctive patterns of intonation, adding new tunes to the old ones.

CHAPTER 9

Styles and strategies

When looking more closely at a particular language, one can see that there are considerable variations in the way it is spoken or written. If the language is spread over a large area, there are usually variations according to the regions where it is spoken. These regional differences may be quite noticeable, as for instance in Britain, or more subtle, as for instance between the different Australian states. We have already mentioned that in some of the New Englishes, regional differences can be noticed. Sometimes they reflect features in the speakers' local languages.

Often, the way people speak or write varies according to their socio-economic status. The speech of the upper middle class, for example, may be quite different from that of the lower middle class or the working class. These different varieties of speech and/or writing within a language are often called *social dialects* or *sociolects*. Very frequently a sociolect also reflects a person's level of education as, naturally, better qualifications often result in better job opportunities.

In the New Englishes, sociolects are even more strongly linked with levels of education than they are in the more established varieties. As many of the New Englishes are still developing varieties, higher levels of education, with English as the medium of instruction, often imply greater proficiency in English; and in some of the New Nations, greater proficiency in English is likely to guarantee occupations with higher pay and more status. However, it would be wrong to say that there is a one-to-one relationship between a sociolect of a speaker of a New English and his or her level of education. Someone with a lower level of English-medium education could have gained greater proficiency in

English by private study or by working in a firm or institution where English is used as the main language of communication. His or her sociolect would be different from someone who had the same level of education but who had taken a low status job where most of the communication was in a local language.

Styles

There is a third type of variation in the speech and writing of a language which has to do with the context in which the language is used. It matters, for example, whether it is a formal situation or an informal one. Different language would be used at a funeral than at the market. It matters, too, what the relationship of the speaker or writer is to the person he or she addresses, e.g. whether it is the boss or a friend. We shall talk about this in more detail when discussing some of the discourse structures in the New Englishes later in the chapter. This third type of variation in a language is variation in *style*.

In the more established varieties of English, speakers use a considerable range of styles *within* their sociolect. In other words, as far as speech is concerned, a person always talks in a certain way which may mark him as belonging to a certain region or social class. Within the boundaries of this way of speaking he has a choice of a number of variations, his different styles. A speaker would usually have a range of styles from a very informal to a very formal style. For example, an educated speaker of British English may use the following requests (according to the situation or the person addressed):

Would you be so kind, Sir, as to let me have the details on the Knox transaction

Could you please give me the details on the Knox transaction, Mr Smith

Dawkins, could I have all you've got on the Knox deal, please

Bob, let's have all that stuff on the Knox deal

In a more informal style, sentences are generally shorter and the vocabulary used is either more simple or more 'racy'.

An interesting factor about the New Englishes is that most of them have not yet developed a stylistic range *within* sociolects. What this means is that speakers of the New Englishes have to use their 'best'

English for formal occasions and use 'something else' for more informal occasions. Four main possibilities are available and, according to the region and the background against which the New Englishes have developed, speakers have made use of these possibilities. Naturally, they are not all mutually exclusive and there are certain overlaps. However, the general pattern is that the educated speaker of the New English uses a higher sociolect as formal style and

(1) *either* uses a lower sociolect as informal style
   (e.g. speakers of Singapore English, some speakers of Malaysian English)

(2) *or* uses the local creole or pidgin as informal style
   (e.g. speakers of Caribbean English, Papua New Guinean English, some speakers of Nigerian English)

(3) *or* uses a special type of mix-mix, this is a mixture between the New English and the local language, as informal style
   (e.g. speakers of Philippine English)

(4) *or* uses one of the local languages in informal situations
   (e.g. speakers of some of the African Englishes)

As we have said already, these four possibilities are not always mutually exclusive. For example, in an informal situation at home, an educated Singaporean may talk in a Chinese dialect to her parents but talk in a lower sociolect of Singapore English to her brothers and sisters.

If an educated speaker of a New English switches to a lower sociolect for his informal style, he may, for example, more frequently use aspect markers instead of marking his verbs for past tense and mark the plural of nouns less frequently.[1] He may also use more of the words and expressions from the local languages, some of which we have mentioned in Chapter 6.

For example, an educated Singaporean may say at a formal meeting:

I think it's almost one now. Shall we adjourn now for lunch and discuss the matter afterwards?

but he may say to his colleagues:

Wah one o'clock already. Time really fly man! Maybe we makan first lah.

The use of the local pidgin or creole as an informal variety for educated speakers of New English is generally more widespread than some speakers are willing to admit. All over the English-speaking part of the

Caribbean, English is 'the code for signalling formality, social distance, greater importance in the social hierarchy, education. . .'[2] but the Creole, the *sweet talk*, is used when talking to close friends. In the words of an educated speaker from Tobago,[3]

> And you would meet an educated Tobagonian who speaks fairly well, as I'm speaking with you, and nevertheless, when I'm with my friends on the beach I'll say 'How you boy? How you keepin'?' without going for the formal English all the time. It's not sweet enough. And the school children as they talk along the road, they wouldn't speak standard English. When they go to school, in the classroom, teachers insist that they speak properly. But out of the classroom, they go back to their own jolly good way of life. It is so much sweeter.

This second 'sweeter' language is a Creole language.

Bickerton[4] quotes a speaker from Guyana who uses sentences such as (1) to strangers and (2) to intimate friends:

(1)   Well J___ went away but B___ has a boy there who was working with J___ for years, over twenty years and left J___

(2)   mi main tel mi a i – if na i, a hu mi mos se? a i sen am, mi main gi ma a i.
       (I think it was him – if it wasn't him, who could it have been? It was him sent it, I think it was him)

Example (2) is a variety of Guyanian Creole.

Often, of course, speakers will not always vary as drastically as in this example. Educated Jamaicans, Guyanians, Tobagonians, for example, may have more or fewer Creole terms or structures in their English speech, depending on the situation of the person addressed or even the topic they are talking about.[5] Usually, the more informal the situation, the more prominent is the use of the Creole.

In the Philippines, on the other hand, educated speakers of English use a particular type of mixture of Pilipino (Tagalog) and English, at times referred to as mix-mix, in less formal situations. This is quite different from a speaker mixing in words and expressions from a local language because his English is not good enough. Many speakers who use mix-mix could equally well talk to each other in English but they use both languages, switching backward and forward, often several times within one sentence.

This type of language, or *code mixing*, is described by Gumperz[6]

Speakers communicate fluently, maintaining an even flow of talk.
No hesitation pauses, changes in sentence rhythm, pitch or level
of intonation contour mark the shift in the code. There is nothing
in the exchange as a whole to indicate that the speakers don't
understand each other. Apart from the alternation itself, the
passages have all the earmarks of ordinary conversations in a
single language.

It is interesting that in mix-mix, a rather formal type of English is
often combined with a more colloquial style of the local language.
This can be seen in the excerpt from a story in a Philippine newspaper[7]
where the writer obviously wished to achieve a certain rapport between
himself and his readers:

Tipong heavy and intro ko, pero it happened one night dito sa
destitute place namin. Ganito iyon, listen carefully. Around ten
thirty in the evening nang dumating sa bahay ni utol ang kanyang
kubrador ng Jai-Alai na si Dencio.
(It looks like my introduction is heavy (too serious), but it
happened one night here at our destitute place. It was like this,
listen carefully. (It was) around ten thirty in the evening when
Dencio, his Jai-Alai bookie, arrived at the house of Brother (my
brother).)

In the Philippines, mix-mix may also appear in popular advertisements as in this one from PANORAMA (only an excerpt is given)
which encourages the reader to become a dealer of Pops Ice Buko
(frozen coconut shavings on sticks):

Sa dealer, we can also provide a freezer na pinakamura ang
halaga at pinakamadali ang terms. Mapapakinabangan ng malaki
ang freezer na ito sa inyong tindahan o grocery. Susuportahan pa
kayo ng free advertising materials upang lalong lumaki ang inyong
benta. Samantalahin ang pagkakataong dagdagan ng libo-libo ang
inyong kita. Be a Pops Dealer in your area. Inquire now.

In these cases, Philippine English would be considered too formal
and not nearly as effective as the mixed variety. Richards[8] quotes an
educated Filipino as saying:

If I go into an office in Manila and try to get a clerk to do something for me, to get a document or some such thing, if I speak to
the clerk in English, the situation becomes over formal; if I mix-
mix the situation is easier to handle

In the fourth possibility which we have mentioned, the educated speakers of the New English would have only a relatively formal or semi-formal style in their New English and would not use English but rather their local languages in all informal situations.

There are other differences between the New Englishes and 'older' Englishes. There are, for instance, words and constructions which in the 'older' Englishes belong mainly to a formal written language or to a very formal spoken style. In the New Englishes, these are often used in casual conversation or writing. The following are examples taken from fairly informal conversations:

from Philippine English:

Every family that I have *encountered*

from West African English:

So English *predominates*, I would say

You send it to someone you *cherish*

from East African English:

I have never *witnessed* any of these expressions

I didn't *undergo* the kind of education that I'm describing here

So you will *encounter* English very often

from Singapore English:

I *converse* English with my parents

We do *encounter* things like taking payment
(the speaker did not refer to bribes but to regular payments made by customers)

I *occupy* one room with my two sisters

So far I *witness* a few (weddings)

You flew here, I *presume*

In some of the New Englishes, e.g. in Indian English, there is a preference for lengthy constructions, bookish vocabulary and exaggerated forms which make even a formal style appear 'more formal' to a speaker of another variety of English, e.g.[9]

I am bubbling with zeal and enthusiasm to serve as a research assistant

I wish to express my overflowing devotion to him

Our country is facing at the moment multitudinous hydra-headed problems

The same can be found in African English, as this excerpt from a headmaster's letter to a student shows[10]

Your deportment of late has been so unruly that you are now deemed a misfit in this academic institution. With effect from the issue of this letter of admonishment, I expect you to shrink your tentacles within the boundaries of learning.

There are several reasons for this 'overformalizing':

(1)   A lack of knowledge of other words or structures, that is of a less formal way of saying it.

(2)   An attitude that formal English is the only *good* English and that everything else is *bad* English, often referred to as *slang*. One may use this slang with one's friends, but *naturally* to an outsider one would use 'formal good English'. Both of these reasons are tied up with what has been taught in schools, teachers' and lecturers' attitudes and overall educational policies. We shall talk more about this in the next chapter.

(3)   The third reason is the influence of the background culture which may demand certain stylistic devices in letter writing or a set form of address to strangers and superiors. More than this, the background culture may demand a certain basic attitude from the speaker or writer in a number of situations.

Mehrotra,[9] for instance, comments on a humility and, to the outsider, excessive modesty which is part of Indian culture and which is reflected in Indian English. For example, in many varieties of English the writer may express his thanks for having received a favour or for services rendered but in Indian English thanks may be given 'in situations where a favour or benefit is absolutely out of the question',[9] e.g.

I hope I satisfy your requirements. Thanking you

I promise to take up the task with complete sincerity and dedication. Thanking you

I offer myself as a candidate for the post of Research Assistant.
Thanking you

A typical formal letter of a writer of some of the New Englishes,
e.g. Indian or African English, may have an extremely deferential
vocabulary based on the politeness formulas of the background language
of the writer, and 'an abundant use of blessings in the opening and
concluding paragraphs. If the writer is senior in age, the use of blessings
would seem excessive to a person who is not part of the culture. One
might find mentioned names of gods who will bless the receiver of the
letter.'[11]

An interesting factor is the constant use in some of the New Englishes
of some colloquial expressions in formal or semi-formal speech. Two
terms which are fairly widely spread among the New Englishes are
hubby and *missus*.

In some of the established varieties of English, *hubby* (for *husband*)
conjures up the image of the middle-aged, often friendly but also hen-
pecked male. It would generally not be used by upper middle and
upper class women when referring to their husbands. It is rarely used
as an address form. In some of the New Englishes this is not so.

For example:

Hubby, hubby come here!

a smart young Singaporean called out to her husband.

The term *missus* in British English is predominantly a social marker.
It is usually considered typical of lower class speech, e.g.

Me 'n the *missus* went there

This is not so in some of the New Englishes. In Ghanaian English, for
example, it is widely used but 'restricted as a mode of address and
reference for a woman (usually literate) married in a church or at a
registry office, according to Western European customs. The term
does not apply to women married according to native Ghanaian
custom.'[12]

In Indian English, the term is widely used without social or stylistic
restrictions. Subrahmaniam[13] explains that to some educated people
the term *my wife* sounds too possessive and the term *Mrs X* too remote
and that the compromise is *my Mrs* which is 'absolutely Indian and
widely used over the country'.

Many Singaporeans feel *missus* to be more polite than *wife*. In fact, a number of Singaporeans expressed the opinion that *wife* was not a very courteous word to use if one was enquiring about a man's spouse. Therefore one of the writers was asked politely:

And how is your *missus* today, Sir? and

We would like your *missus* to come too

Communication strategies

The term *strategies* may suggest the deliberate planning of an action. Naturally, in communication, people may sometimes deliberately plan what type of language to use but usually language choice in most situations is more or less subconscious. It is often based on certain social and/or cultural norms and, at times, on the speaker's or writer's individual preferences. He or she uses language as the situation demands. Actually, in order to 'select' appropriate language for the occasion, a speaker has to take into account a number of factors, for example

(1) where he is, e.g. in a school, the office, a church or the market place;
(2) whom he is talking to, e.g. a stranger or a friend;
(3) and if he knows the person, what his relationship to the person is, e.g. friend, colleague, older relative, superior;
(4) what topic he is talking about, e.g. a funeral or last night's party.

All these factors would determine what type of language the speaker or writer would choose in order to communicate with the other person. They would determine how formal or informal he needed to be, e.g. what sentence structures and vocabulary he would use. Naturally, there are also personal factors, e.g. whether his relationship to the other person was friendly, hostile or just neutral. It would also matter whether the two had certain past experiences in common that could be presupposed, e.g.

What about that handbag, did you buy it after all?

or whether they shared some common general knowledge about the world around them:

Heavens, you look like Marcel Marceau!

would mean little to anyone who didn't know who Marcel Marceau was.

A child acquiring English as a native language in any cultural setting, e.g. in Britain, Australia or the United States, would also acquire the ability to use language in context, what Hymes[14] has called *communicative competence*. A child growing up in a New Nation as a speaker of a New English and using this English from an early age would also quickly acquire a type of communicative competence. This competence may include the knowledge of when to use the New English and when to use the local language. For example, an English-speaking Singaporean Chinese would know precisely when to use formal Singapore English, when to use colloquial Singapore English, when to use Mandarin and when to use Hokkien. The communicative competence of a speaker of a New English may differ quite considerably from that of a speaker of a more established variety as their respective social and cultural backgrounds may be vastly different.

Forms of address

Some languages have a complex system of address forms, according to the age and status of the addressee and the relationship he has to the speaker or writer. The English address forms appear relatively simple to an outsider but often there is quite a complexity in their use.

The use of the first name has become more common. In writing it is now used more frequently, together with the surname, in addressing letters, e.g. *Mary Smith* instead of Mrs M. Smith, Miss M. Smith or M/s M. Smith. First names are probably now the most frequent mode of address; they may even be used to perfect strangers, particularly in face-to-face communication. Australians seem to be leading the way in this practice:

Hi, meet Bill and Mary
I'd like you to meet Peter, etc.

It is quite possible to live for half a year in a new environment and be on very friendly terms with one's neighbours without knowing their surname. When the first name is offered as an address form, e.g. 'Please call me Jean' and the offer is not taken up, this may cause offence to the other person.

Speakers of New Englishes are usually reluctant to use first names in addressing someone unless they know the other person well. Their background cultures often demand respect for those in certain positions, for older persons and for strangers. The idea of addressing their boss or lecturer as Bill or Fred, Mary or Betty seems alien to them.

We have already mentioned the use of kinship terms as forms of address in Chapter 6. This is common in a number of Englishes. Carr[15] mentions the use of the word *bla* or *blala* (brother) in Hawaiian English:

> Ey, bla! uttered by a member of the peer group may be a warm and affectionate greeting. . . (bla and blala are) used by, and for, Island-born men and boys, whether relatives or friends. In the Hawaiian language, the term parallel to *brother* may include a male first, second or third cousin.

Akere[16] talks about the use of *Daddy, Mommy, Uncle* and *Auntie* outside the family:

> A common feature of usage among women and young girls in government offices, in the market place and among street traders in urban centres is the use of the terms *Daddy* and *Mommy* as address terms for adult men and women. . . . Street hawkers and market traders wanting to sell their wares use the forms frequently for car owners who stop by to buy some commodities at the road side. Such usage carries deferential overtones in relation to age differences and status. Immediate bosses in their places of work get addressed as either *Daddy* or *Mommy* by subordinate young officers.

The use of titles is common in many of the New Englishes, e.g. Nigerian English:[16]

> *Alhaji Chief Doctor* + Last Name (for a person who is a medical doctor or Ph.D. holder who has taken a chieftaincy title and has also made a Muslim pilgrimage to Mecca and Medina)

Singaporean salesgirls, especially those who are Chinese-medium educated, often use *Aunty* and *Miss*, e.g.

> Anything else, *Aunty?* (to an older woman)
> *Miss* ah, anything else? (to a younger woman)

Chinese-medium educated young salesmen commonly address younger girls as *sister*, e.g.

Hello *sister*, come into the shop and look lah!

Greetings and leave takings

When people meet, there are usually certain expressions which begin
and end the meeting. Unlike the rest of the conversation, expressions
of greetings and leave takings are usually fairly predictable. They belong
to a small group of expressions and their order is more or less fixed, so
that they have sometimes even been called *greeting rituals* or *leave-
taking rituals.* For example, a common greeting ritual in Australian
English would be:

A: How are ya?
B: Fine.
A: That's good.

If B had answered 'Rotten' or 'I'm not feeling too good today' he
would be stepping outside the ritual and starting a proper conversation.
There is, of course, some variation in these rituals according to the
situation and the age and relationship of the people who meet, e.g.

(1) A: Well, how nice to meet you
     B: I haven't seen you for ages

(2) A: Hi
     B: Hi

In the New Englishes, speakers may begin a greeting or end a leave-
taking with a word from the background language. Two well-known
expressions are the Hawaiian *aloha* and the East African *(H)ujambo*?
Aloha, which is widely used in Hawaii for hello or goodbye, even by
people of a non-Hawaiian background, often signals friendliness and
goodwill. The kiSwahili greeting *(H)ujambo*? 'Are you well?' literally
means 'Is there no problem?' 'Are you without a problem?' The answer
would be *Sijambo* 'There is no problem.' Educated speakers of East
African English say that they may start off with the *Hujambo*? –
Sijambo exchange and then may continue the conversation in English.

On the other hand, some Ghanaian speakers of English may finish a
leave-taking in English with

O.K. *abanabo* (or *awanabu*) 'I'll see you again'

literally 'one will see you' or 'you'll be seen'. The 'again' is implied.

Some expressions for greetings and leave-takings are direct translations from the background languages, e.g.

from Sri Lankan English:[17]

> So how?
> (Sinhala: *itin kohomədə?*)

and as a farewell

> I'll go and come
> (Sinhala.   *maŋ gihilla ennaŋ*)

from Nigerian English[18] as a greeting

> You're enjoying?
> (Yoruba: *Eku igbadun*)
> literally 'I greet you as you enjoy yourself'

A Singaporean or Malaysian Chinese may tell a departing guest:

> Walk slowly ho!
> (Hokkien: Bān bān kià^n hó^n)
> literally 'slow slow walk' (*hó^n* is a particle expressing concern)

He or she may greet someone, particularly near a meal time, with

Have you eaten already?
Had your lunch/dinner already?
(Hokkien: Chiảh (pá) bē?)
              'Eat   full not yet'
(Malay: Sudah makan?) literally 'finish eating'

This greeting may cause some misunderstanding if it is made to an outsider. A speaker of another variety of English would most likely take it as a straightforward request for information and, on answering in the negative, would usually expect an invitation to lunch or dinner.

Some greetings, although influenced by the background languages and cultures, are close in structure and meaning to those used in more established varieties, though their range often differs somewhat, e.g.

from West African English:[19]

How? How now?

from East African English:[20]

Are you all right?

For some speakers of African English *thank you* is used as a reply to *goodbye*.

For the younger generation of speakers of the New Englishes, the nearly universal *Hi* seems to have become very popular as a form of greeting and O.K. as a form of leave-taking, e.g. from Singapore English:

Hi, just come ah?
So O.K. lah

and on the telephone: O.K. lah. See you some time, lah.

Traditionally, in many cultures, greeting and leave-taking rituals were longer and more complex. One enquired after the health and well-being not only of the person one met but also of his family. Some of these rituals are still used in some of the background languages and may be reflected in the greeting exchanges in English.

A young Nigerian talked about the greeting ritual of some older Nigerians:

They say: 'How are you? How is. . .?
Is there any bad news?
No bad news.
How is news?
Good news.
How are your children?'

And they go on and on. Then they start talking properly.

Responses to questions

An interesting difference between the established varieties of English and some of the New Englishes is the way a response is made to certain negative questions or statements. In the established varieties of English if A asks a question like:

Didn't you get to the university yesterday?

and B wants to indicate that he or she *didn't* go, the reply would usually include *No*, e.g.

No, I didn't.

157

Similarly if the person spoken to wanted to show agreement with a remark like:

I suppose you won't be going there after all

the answer would usually start with *No*, e.g.

No, I suppose not

However, in some of the New Englishes, the appropriate response would include *Yes*, e.g.

from Indian English:[20]

Q: Didn't I see you yesterday in college?
A: Yes, you didn't see me yesterday in college.

Q: You have no objection?
A: Yes, I have no objection.

from African English:

Q: Hasn't the President left for Nairobi yet?
A: Yes, the President hasn't left for Nairobi yet.[21]

Q: So you didn't get to see much of Singapore?
A: Yeah. I didn't see much, yes.

The speaker agrees with the fact that he 'hasn't seen much of Singapore'.

This logic in answering negative questions can also be seen in a number of African languages, e.g.

from Lingala (a Bantu language)[21]

Q: Boliyákí te? Didn't you (pl.) eat?
A: Ee. (Toliyákí te) Yes. (We didn't eat)

from Hausa:[22]

Q:	bai zo ba?	Hasn't he come?
A(1)	i	Yes (i.e. what you have said is right: he has not come)
A(2)	a'a	No (i.e. what you have said is wrong: he has come)

In Singapore English and Malaysian English, responses such as *can*, *also can* and *can also* are considered quite polite in certain situations, e.g.

Q: D'you want another cup of coffee?
A: Can
(This is considered preferable to 'yes, I will' or 'yes, please' as it suggests here 'I don't want to put you to a lot of trouble' *Can* may also express agreement with the other person's suggestion.)

The response *I don't mind* has a more positive and definite meaning than in other varieties of English. In British English, it usually means 'I have no objection', e.g. 'I don't mind waiting'. For a Malaysian or a Singaporean it has more the meaning of 'I should like to', e.g.

A: Would you like to come to my house for dinner on Tuesday?
B: I don't mind.

B is not showing indifference or absence of enthusiasm but is politely accepting the invitation.[23]

There is, of course, a somewhat dated British English expression that has a similar meaning, e.g.

Would you like another piece of cake?
Oh, I don't mind if I do.

Reactions to events

In West African English, the reaction to any surprising event whether good or bad may be *wonderful!* which simply expresses the speaker's amazement:[22] e.g.

A: He died yesterday morning
B: Wonderful!

And throughout African English, we can find the use of *sorry!* as an exclamation of sympathy although the speaker need not have been responsible for what happened to the other person. An educated speaker of West African English explained:

You trip. Everyone knows what it feels like to trip, so you sympathize with the person straight away and you say *Oh sorry*. It has nothing to do with apologizing. The person means 'I'm sorry that you have hurt your foot; I'm sorry *for you*.' If you are responsible for something, you would not just say one word. You would make it very clear that you apologize.

She tells about her primary school teacher:

> She hurt herself. The whole class would say: 'Oh sorry, Miss James!' She would say: 'Don't say *sorry* when it's not your fault.' We couldn't understand. We thought 'These people are very strange.'

It is fascinating to listen to and compare different exchanges that take place when people talk to each other. Unfortunately, because of lack of space, we can give only one example here. It is a conversation between two young women in a department store, speaking colloquial Singapore English. It shows the use of discourse particles to convey certain information, attitudes and create a feeling of informality and solidarity. It also shows question structures and the *can also* response as well as the use of expressions and structures which we have mentioned earlier in the book:

(A is trying on a pair of shoes)
B: Can fit or not? Not bad what? Cheap what?
   (*what* expresses here 'you really must agree with me')
   Can buy lah!
(B tries on a pair)
A: Eh, can fit your leg.
   (No distinction is made in Chinese between *feet* and *legs*)
B: The leg down there a bit uncomfortable
   (Looks at some other shoes) This one don't have less, ah?
   (meaning 'There isn't any discount on these?')
   I don't want to buy.
A: We walk down lah.
   (meaning 'let's use the staircase instead of the lift')
B: Can also.

CHAPTER 10

The teacher's dilemma

Which is the correct view? A or B?:

A: . . . the heretical tenet I feel I must take exception to is the idea that it is best, in a country where English is not spoken natively but is widely used as a medium of instruction, to set up the local variety of English as the ultimate model to be imitated by those learning the language.[1]

B: It is obvious that in the Third World Countries the choice of functions and models of English has to be determined on a pragmatic basis, keeping in view the local conditions and needs. It will, therefore, be appropriate that the native speakers of English abandon the attitude of linguistic chauvinism and replace it with an attitude of linguistic tolerance. The strength of the English language is in presenting the *Americanness* in its American variety, and the *Englishness* in its British variety. Let us therefore appreciate and encourage the Third World varieties of English too.[2]

This is the teacher's dilemma! Those doing research into the English spoken in the teacher's New Nation. Tell the teacher that a variety or several varieties of a New English *exist*. The teacher knows that the New English exists, because he or she uses it. However, the teacher is often told by the authorities that it *must not exist* and that it is up to him or her to 'teach it away' and that it is his or her fault that it is still there! The blame is often handed down through the hierarchy. University lecturers blame secondary teachers for the students' 'bad English' and secondary teachers blame primary teachers. The poor primary teachers cannot usually blame the parents because a local language rather than English may be spoken in the home. So they are stuck with the blame. The same process, incidentally, is going on in countries where more established varieties of English are spoken, such as Britain and Australia. The only difference is that primary school teachers can blame the parents and TV.

It all starts off with the concept of *standard*. The term standard can be used in two ways. A standard may be (a) considered an ideal towards which one may strive but may not necessarily reach or, on the other hand, (b) it may be considered as one of a pair which signals *right* or *wrong*. This means that standard is considered to be above a rigid line — anything below this line is *sub-standard*.

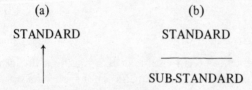

The view expressed by (b) is rather unrealistic. Language is a part of human behaviour and therefore a part of real life. In real life there is often no clear-cut dichotomy. After all, even between black and white there are many shades of grey!

It is because of the (b) interpretation of the term standard that it has at times a negative and rather over-prescriptive flavour. It need not have such a flavour if we look at meaning (a). Sometimes, other words have been used for meaning (a), such as *model*.[2]

There is no doubt that all language teachers need a model of the language they are going to teach. Before we look more closely at possible models, we should like to introduce another term: *norm*. Sometimes norm is used synonymously with standard. We shall use it here for guidelines for language behaviour, any human behaviour for that matter, in certain situations. All norms are bound by the context of the situation. There are norms for behaviour, including language behaviour, in formal situations and those for informal situations, norms for using language in writing, formal or informal, and those for using language in speech. Instead of using terms such as *correct* and *incorrect*, we shall use *appropriate* and *inappropriate*. Something that may be quite inappropriate language behaviour in formal writing may be perfectly appropriate, even quite desirable, in informal speech.

External standards

In colonial times, the model for English teaching was either British or American English and it remained this way, at least officially, when the colonies became new nations. The norms which were presented to the learners of English were essentially *written* norms. Spoken norms were rarely introduced. Any dialogues in English language textbooks were usually so stilted and unreal that they would have been considered inappropriate for any situation, formal or informal, in a native English context. When finally more enlightened textbook material appeared which introduced situations, formal and informal, which were real, or at least close-to-reality, another problem arose.

To the learners of English in the New Nations and to those who were already partially speakers of the New English, some of these situations reflecting British or American life were quite unreal. They did not reflect their cultural settings, their norms of behaviour and, above all, they did not reflect the norms of use of the New English. There is a difference between learning English in a country such as Germany, where it will remain a foreign language, and learning English in a country where it is used not only as the medium of instruction but also in various activities outside the classroom and where it has slowly established itself as a variety in its own right.

Local standards

What would be the problems if the model for teaching English in a New Nation were a local one? 'Ha!' the critics would say triumphantly to researchers who have attempted to describe a New English. 'So you want our teachers to teach our colloquial variety at school. How absurd!' Yes, it is indeed absurd and nobody would advocate such a view. The simple reason for this is that a colloquial variety, whether of an established or of a developing English, need not be taught. People know it already or children acquire it quite naturally in the home, from the neighbours or in the school playground.

With a New English, two perspectives have to be considered at practically the same time, and they are often confused. On the one hand, a more established New English can be considered a *functional variety*[3] which is used for many communicative purposes in the socio-cultural life of the community. It has its different sociolects which, as we have mentioned earlier, are often related to the educational background of the speakers. Its speakers practise different language behaviour in different situations, using a more colloquial, localized form of language for informal situations and a different, less localized form for more formal situations. Just as colloquial forms of the more established Englishes are considered appropriate for certain situations, so too should colloquial forms of the New Englishes be considered appropriate for informal situations in the socio-cultural context of the New Nation.

However, many of the New Englishes are also *developing* varieties. This means that they have speakers who are also learners. Children who speak other languages in the home have to be 'taught' English as a subject. And, as we have said before, when any language is taught, a teaching model is required. If a local teaching model were to be chosen, it would need to be based on the English used by the educated speakers of the New Nation − not only their formal written English but their whole range of situational language behaviour from formal to informal in speech and writing.

There are three main problems, by no means insurmountable, that would have to be seriously considered if a local model were to be adopted as a teaching model. They are:

(1) How to define *educated* speakers of a New English.
(2) How to show the systematicity of the New English.
(3) What to use as informal spoken style in teaching materials.

Educated speakers

Who are the *educated* speakers of the New English? What is often implied by this term is a type of social elite. In the new nations this often means those who also have higher levels of education. Their English, in its formal style, would be the closest to an 'international' type of English. The question is: What is the dividing line between being *educated* and not being educated? Boadi, for example, deals with this question when he talks about English in Ghana:[4]

A few years ago most people who had spent eight to ten years at elementary school could get a reasonably good job because they could claim that they were educated. Now the position is different; present-day primary school learners and certain

categories of GCE 'O' level holders are said for many purposes
to be 'illiterate'. In a desperate effort to look for the educated
norm, some people have turned to university graduates and
sections of the community who have professional qualifications.
The difficulty with this criterion is that it leaves out a relatively
large section whose use of English is undoubtedly what one would
like to describe as educated.

If one wanted to establish a teaching model based on the usage of
educated speakers, there would be an obvious need in a New Nation to
consider where the cut-off point for educated speakers would be. It would
matter here to what extent a New English was still a developing variety,
that is a learner's language, and to what extent it had reached the level
of being a functional variety.

One would also have to consider to what extent social and economic
factors should be included when selecting the group of educated
speakers. In our investigations of Singapore and Malaysian English,[5] for
example, we found that what mattered was not only the level of
education but also the social background of the speaker. And what was
particularly important was the type of work situation; that is whether
or not the main language of communication there was English.

There is also the question of *where* these educated speakers are
educated. Bamgbose,[6] when talking about Nigerian English, says:

The subjective element again enters: Whose usage is to be
accepted? I hasten to suggest that it should not be that of the
purist (who does not believe in a Nigerian English anyway) nor
that of the foreign-educated elite. . . . The natural and spontaneous
usage of the locally educated Nigerian user of English is a more
reliable guide to the identification of typical Nigerian usage.

Of course, the borderline between foreign-educated or not is a fluid
one. Someone may have gone abroad to further his or her education
after having obtained a local university degree and may return to his or
her own country, essentially as a speaker of the New English. Others
may have been sent abroad by their parents to finish their secondary
schooling, have stayed on to finish their tertiary education and may
return as speakers of other more established varieties. This is relatively
rare. Usually, traces of the local variety remain and are immediately
reinforced once a speaker has returned to his or her own country.

A third point to consider is whether or not some of the educated speakers of the New English are *native* speakers. It all depends on the interpretation of the concept native speaker. 'It was stated by a teacher in East Africa that . . . for English the accepted standard is the speech (or writing) of well educated native speakers.'[7] Obviously, he took it to mean 'Englishmen, Americans, Australians, etc.' However, if it is taken, as it usually is, to mean someone who acquires the language as his or her first language when a child and uses it exclusively, or at least as one of his or her main languages of communication, then some of the New Englishes certainly do have native speakers. For example, in Singapore and Malaysia, Eurasians, many Christian Indians and some Straits-born Chinese speak Singapore English or Malaysian English as their *native* language, that is the *first* language acquired as children from their parents. One may use an even wider definition of native speaker. In the words of Tay:[8]

(1)   A 'native speaker' of English is not identified only by virtue of his birthright. He need not be from the U.K., U.S., Australia, New Zealand, or one of the traditionally 'native speaking' countries.

(2)   A 'native speaker' of English who is not from one of the countries mentioned above is one who learns English in childhood *and* continues to use it as his dominant language *and* has reached a certain level of fluency. All three conditions are important. . . .

Tay continues to say that:

According to our definition of 'native speaker', there are many more 'native speakers' of English in Singapore than are normally identified in census reports. One problem with using census data in identifying a person's native language in a multi-ethnic country is that a person may identify Hokkien, Cantonese, or Tamil as his mother tongue or native language because that is his ethnic language. . . .

Systematicity

If it were desirable to use the language of the educated group as a teaching model, and *if* this group had been defined, then a whole lot of work would lie ahead for the linguists and educationists of the New

Nation. Teachers cannot teach in a vacuum. They do not want a model that may be suggested to them but which is nothing more than a vague outline. They need textbooks, readers, syllabuses, etc. based on the local standard, but above all they need *systematicity*. They need some kind of model to which they can refer, a model which tells them what to regard as a 'learner's mistake' and what to consider as a legitimate feature of the educated variety of the New English. Such a model, although it is by no means impossible, is a big undertaking. It would involve more than just haphazardly collecting 'deviations' or 'errors' in speech or writing, even on a large scale. It would involve a thorough and systematic analysis of the speech and writing of a large and representative group of educated speakers. It would also involve large-scale acceptability testing similar to what has been carried out on more established varieties. The only way to show that a language feature is not an idiosyncratic learner's error but part of the language system of a New English is to prove, statistically (a) that it is used frequently and systematically by its speakers and (b) that they know how to use it, where and to whom.

Those involved with teaching and investigating English in their own New Nation have realized some of these problems. We shall give here a selection of comments from a number of different nations:

from Ghana:[9]

> What we must look for are the broad similarities which set
> together users of English belonging to the various professions
> and levels of education. . . . It is very likely that there are wide-
> spread peculiarities in their use of vocabulary, idiom, grammar,
> intonation and rhythm which these groups of educated Ghanaians
> share in common.

from Nigeria:[10]

> In a recent detailed study of certain characteristics of Nigerian
> English Adetugbo (1977a) concludes that English language usage
> in Nigeria has its own characteristics that set it apart from any
> native variety. The differentiating features occur at various levels
> of grammatical structure. . . . They also occur at the level of
> phonology realization and semantic interpretation. Adetugbo
> asserts that these features are no mere deviations from the norms
> of the native speaker's standard English, but that they constitute
> features that characterize standard Nigerian English.

from Sri Lanka:[11]

> (The writer is referring to educated Lankan English)
> It has its own well-articulated rules, which differentiate it in
> certain important ways from the original model (with which, need-
> less to say, it nevertheless continues to have a great deal in common).
> These rules at the same time give the speakers an intuitive in-
> dependent standard of judgement in terms of which certain forms
> and expressions may be characterized as being either errors (so that
> they would have no role in defining the system of Lankan English)
> or markers of sociolinguistically definable sub-varieties of Lankan
> English itself.

from the Philippines:[12]

> . . .research should be done towards a description of Standard
> Philippine English. Such questions as: Is there a sociolectal cline
> from basilect to acrolect in Philippine English, or is there simply
> the polarization between educated Philippine English and idio-
> syncratic Philippine English? Should educated Philippine English
> with its generally standard English features, with some minor
> deviations in idiom and grammar and phonology be given the label
> 'Standard Philippine English'? . . . Should the exonormative
> standard of General American English continue being maintained,
> or should a switch be made to Standard Philippine English as the
> norm?

from Singapore:

> Research on Singapore English, notably by Platt and Weber (1980),
> Tay (1979) and Richards (1979) have demonstrated that SE
> (Singapore English) is a distinctive variety different from Standard
> British English (SBrE), from other native 'Englishes' such as
> American or Australian English as well as from non-native varieties
> such as Indian or Pilipino English. Platt and Weber (1980) make
> three important observations about SE: (1) that there is a sur-
> prising amount of system within SE and that it is becoming in-
> creasingly similar even when spoken by Singaporeans of different
> ethnic origins (2) that the SE speech continuum, and to some
> extent written SE, has an acrolectal 'high' or prestige sub-variety,
> upper middle and lower middle mesolectal sub-varieties and a
> 'low' basilectal sub-variety, and (3) that these sub-varieties

correspond to the speaker-user's educational level and socio-economic background[13]

and

An exonormative standard (standard from abroad) for Singapore is clearly impracticable for a number of reasons. First of all, no single exonormative standard of English can adequately fulfil the many functions served by English in Singapore: as an official language, language of education, working language, lingua franca, expression of national identity, and as an international language (Tay 1982:51). Second, the 'English-speaking' environment provided by foreigners is very mixed. As Platt and Weber (1980:197) point out, the popular imported television programmes and 'imported' teachers exemplify not a single exonormative variety of English but a whole range such as American, Scottish, Irish, North of England and Australia. To advocate a single exonormative standard of English for Singapore would be unwise as it would not be sufficiently backed up by the linguistic environment. To advocate several exonormative standards would be impracticable because of time constraints; the burden of learning two languages is heavy enough for the average learner. Third, the average educated Singaporean, including the language teacher, rejects an exonormative variety at least in spoken English because he wants to sound like a Singaporean.[14]

Informal spoken styles

In countries such as Britain and Australia, it has recently been the practice for writers of textbooks and readers used in schools to use fairly colloquial language in some of the dialogues, particularly those which take place in informal situations. If the language of educated local speakers were to be accepted as a teaching model it would have to be realized that educated speakers of the New Englishes often use either a lower sociolect, a creole, a pidgin or a local language as their informal style (see Chapter 9). This would be perfectly appropriate within the social and cultural setting of the speech community but how acceptable would it be in teaching materials? If one wanted to give reality and vitality to textbook dialogues and dialogues in readers, would it be possible, or even desirable, to

(a)   use a lower sociolect?

(b)   use a local pidgin or creole?

What would one do in areas where, in more informal situations, the local languages were used? It would hardly be possible to use the local languages or even a local lingua franca to represent the dialogue in English language textbooks and readers. On the other hand, the use of overformal styles in dialogues may appear unrealistic and unacceptable to the students, particularly those who are somewhat familiar with other alternatives in real life situations. These considerations could prove to be a real problem if a local model were to be adopted for English language teaching purposes.

Attitudes

As an answer to the question: 'When is a local form of English suitable for ELT (English Language Teaching) purposes?' Strevens[15] says that a local form must exist and that it must be 'felt by the local speech community to be a desirable form'.

The question of whether or not a local model would be acceptable to the speakers of a particular New English or whether, in particular, it would be acceptable as a model for teaching English is an extremely difficult question to answer. To the writers' knowledge, no overall survey of this nature has been conducted in any of the New Nations.

Moag[16] says that,

> it is widely acknowledged that speakers of the new Englishes are
> loath to recognize the distinctive character of their English and
> rather insist that they speak one or other of the major ENL (English
> as a Native Language) varieties.

This may be somewhat overstated but it is nevertheless true that quite a few speakers of the New Englishes have this attitude. In a workshop on English language use in Singapore, a speaker with a noticeable Singapore English accent vehemently declared: *I speak RP*. This drew laughter and protest from the British English speakers in the audience.

Why are speakers of the New Englishes reluctant to admit

(a)   that their New English exists
             and/or

(b)   that it could be used as a suitable model within the country?

There are many reasons. It is possible that some of them are not perceptive enough to realize that they speak a different type of English from, for example, that spoken in Britain or America. Bamgbose[6] quotes the example of an important personality who, when told that the university department was interested in research on Nigerian English, commented that it was a waste of time as there was no such thing as Nigerian English. A few minutes later he said, on being interrupted: *let me land* – the Nigerian equivalent of *let me finish*.

Another reason may be a basic language insecurity, brought about by past and present attitudes expressed by native speakers or even by a foreign-educated elite in the New Nation. This often results in attitudes such as: 'The real thing comes from overseas – ours is only second best' curiously mixed with a feeling of 'I don't want to speak like an Englishman. I'm a speaker of a New English which contributes to my identity.' For example:

(1) But the educated Ghanaian would not 'accept' anything other than educated British Standard English.[17]

(2) Most of those who refuse to accept that there is a Nigerian English are genuinely worried about the implication of accepting a Nigerian variety of English as an appropriate model, particularly in language teaching. They fear that, in time, such a variety may degenerate into a different language, like pidgin English.[6]

(3) Why is it necessary to speak English the African way? . . . it is generally argued that it would be desirable for educated Ghanaian users of English to impress their African personality on the language by stripping it of all traces of affectation and artificiality. It is further contended that educated Ghanaians lose some of their African identity in their efforts, in using a language which is alien to them, to ape native speakers.[4]

(4) . . . when one is abroad, in a bus or train or aeroplane and when one overhears someone speaking, one can immediately say this is someone from Malaysia or Singapore. And I should hope that when I'm speaking abroad my countrymen will have no problem recognizing that I am a Singaporean.[18]

When attitudes towards English and a suitable model for English are more systematically examined in a New Nation, it is noticeable that there is by no means a consensus among speakers as to the best English model for their country. When a group of speakers of Caribbean English, Barbadians and Guyanese, were asked to rate their own English as against other Englishes, the following results were obtained (given here in full percentages):[19]

Best variety	Total
	%
Own country	36
Other West Indian	7
Great Britain	31
Other country	5
None	21

In 1975, 700 Indian university students and 125 members of the English teaching staff at Indian universities were asked which model of English they would prefer as a teaching model. They were asked to rank various models of English in order of preference. The first preferences were as follows:[20]

Model	Students	Staff
	%	%
American English	5	3
British English	68	67
Indian English	23	27

In the norm investigations which Platt and Weber carried out among Singapore primary school teachers,[21] 60 per cent wanted a British English model but not all of those who chose it were able to recognize the voices of speakers of educated Southeastern English as *British*. Some labelled them as American or Australian.

Teaching aims

Teaching aims which are often stated with regard to the New Englishes are that the students' English should be 'correct, clear and intelligible'. For the teacher who sits in front of a student's essay holding a red ball-point poised in mid air, this is often a tall order.

Intelligible to whom? To another speaker of the same social class? To a speaker of another social class or to a speaker who uses a regionally different variety of the New English? Or does it mean intelligible to a speaker of another variety of English? The need for a wider intelligibility obviously varies from nation to nation. In Singapore, a commercial and tourist centre, the need for *external* intelligibility with regard to English would obviously be much greater than, for instance, in rural areas of Sri Lanka or Nigeria. The problem of *internal* intelligibility, on the other hand, would be less of a problem in a geographically small nation but may be a real problem in a larger nation such as India.

A test was conducted to measure intelligibility between speakers of Indian English and other speakers of Indian English, and between speakers of Indian English and speakers of other varieties of English.[22] It produced the same (average) result for communication *between* Indians speaking English (74 per cent) as that for communication between Indians and Americans (74 per cent). These figures were somewhat higher than for communication between speakers of Indian English and speakers of RP (educated Southeastern British English (70 per cent)).

Mehrotra mentions in relation to Indian English[23] that regional variations in English speech may hamper intelligibility:

A Bengali speaker once annoyed his Punjabi neighbour by his inquiry: Do you have T.B.? What the speaker actually meant was: Do you have TV? At a Gujarati wedding recently an announcement was heard from the microphone 'The snakes are in the hole'. It created panic among the guests. . . . There was a scramble for the exit until someone explained that the message was 'The snacks are in the hall'.

This demonstrates the problem of intelligibility. Misunderstandings and misconceptions about what is meant do not occur in isolation. They occur in a setting, in a particular situation. *Being intelligible* means being understood by a person or persons 'at a given time in a given situation'.[24] It is interesting that in the above example, the announcement was heard *from the microphone*. This means that there were no additional clues to its meaning. If instead a smiling and relaxed host had spoken the same words, pointing to the hall, the intelligibility of the same statement would have been considerably increased.

Language needs to be viewed not in isolation but *in context.*[25] When is it used? For what purpose? By whom and to whom? Is it written language or spoken language? There is a need to be aware that in face-to-face communication other clues can be given in addition to the utterance itself. There are facial expressions, gestures, even the closeness of the speaker to the person he addresses. If these additional factors are not available, e.g. over the phone or over a public address system, other means need to be employed to achieve the same effect, e.g. tone of voice, intonation, additional verbal clues.

When one looks at language in context, one can see that the aims of intelligibility, clarity and correctness mentioned earlier are wider in scope than might at first have been apparent.

(1) *Intelligibility* includes 'awareness of the situation' and the means at one's disposal to convey a particular message and/ or attitude to another person.

(2) *Clarity* includes an awareness of the other person's ability to understand the message.

(3) *Correctness* would include the concept of 'appropriateness', because what is appropriate in one situation may be quite inappropriate for another situation.

In communicating with speakers of other varieties of English, what matters is often not so much the accent or the structure of the English used but different conventions in communicating. When Gumperz and Roberts[26] talk about 'developing awareness skills for interethnic communication' they say that

> communication difficulties cannot be largely attributed to
> problems of accent or lack of knowledge of the structure of
> English. They stem from different conventions in the use of
> English. People from different cultural backgrounds may speak
> a variety of English characterised by certain conventions. It is when
> attitude and meaning are conveyed through one set of conventions
> and interpreted through another that breakdowns in communication
> may occur.

What about communication *within* a New English? Coming back to our school teacher still sitting with a poised red ballpoint in front of a student's English essay. He or she may be pondering what to do with the sentence:

I finish schooling already

If the essay deals with a description of a local situation and the sentence is used as part of local colloquial speech in a dialogue, then this sentence should be accepted as it is appropriate for the situation. If, however, the title of the essay was 'An Application for a Position' and the writer pretended to apply for a position as a clerk or secretary in a large local firm, then the sentence would need to be changed, not because it is *incorrect* — it may, after all, be an acceptable utterance in the local New English — but because it is totally inappropriate for this formal context.

We shall conclude with two comments. One is by a speaker of British English and one by a speaker of a New English. Both are educated speakers and teachers of English and Linguistics at a tertiary institution in a New Nation. Their comments may help towards solving the 'teacher's dilemma':

> what variety of English should be taught? A lower mesolectal or basilectal form which is fairly widespread as a variety of English used in the home is not acceptable from outside the parameters let us say of Singapore and Malaysia. An acrolectal or at least upper mesolectal is necessary. However, we have seen that it is very likely that the child coming into the school will have probably acquired at best a lower mesolectal form of English. We should consider this as a resource to be exploited not something to be ignored as too non-standard to be of any use. This language resource should be used as the vehicle for learning how to read and write. What we might call the child's transitional competence will not approximate fully with adult speech. With young children we have to listen to what they say and not correct them all the time. . . . For example, if during a story-telling session with pictures a child says: 'Why he go there?', the teacher answers the child's query and does not immediately 'correct' the English. . . . Gradually the child recognizes not only are there different forms but there are also different forms for different situations. You say a thing in this way to a friend but in that way to the School Principal.[27]

and

> The attitude of the English language teacher is important in the Singapore context. He should not condemn features of the basilect as 'substandard' or 'uneducated' but point out that they may be used not only among the uneducated but also by the educated if they wish to mark the dimensions of informality, rapport, solidarity and intimacy (Richards and Tay 1977). Besides, the English language teacher in Singapore should be aware of the great amount of 'lectal switching' that goes on all the time. He will not therefore condemn expressions like 'Stop shaking legs and get back to work la'

as substandard but consider its appropriateness in terms of (a) the formality of the situation (it would be appropriate in an informal but not a formal situation), (b) the participants involved in the communication (it would be appropriate for a Singaporean to talk to another Singaporean like that but not to a foreigner) and (c) the media (it would be appropriate in speech under certain conditions but never in serious writing except in novels which attempt to produce 'colloquial' English).[8]

CHAPTER 11

The writer and the New Englishes

With the spread of English during the colonial era, it gradually came to be recognized as something more than purely utilitarian, something more than a means to gaining a livelihood. Of those who reached higher levels of English-medium education, there must have been some who genuinely enjoyed and admired the literature they read at school, who derived pleasure from Shakespeare, Gibbon, and *Palgrave's Golden Treasury* and who wanted to emulate the writers who were presented to them as models of literary excellence. There were those, too, who wanted to let others know of their own experiences and thoughts, who wanted to make their culture and their society known to the wider world.

In some of the colonies there were those who belonged to cultures with long written literary traditions: Chinese, Indian, Sinhalese and Malay. Some creative writers continued these traditions by writing in Chinese, the various Indian Languages, Sinhala and Malay, whether in the homelands of these languages or in the colonies to which they had migrated, such as Malaya and the Straits Settlements. In other areas, there were traditions of oral literature: in Africa, both West and East, in Papua and New Guinea and in the Caribbean region.

In both types of situation, however, there were those who felt the need to reach out to a wider group than could be reached in the mother tongue of the writers. The obvious choice was English. In the second type of situation, there was, of course, an added reason. It is only comparatively recently that writing systems have been devised for many of the languages spoken in Africa and Papua New Guinea, and the Caribbean creoles had no standardized orthography.

Some writers in nations where New Englishes are spoken use a variety of English which gives few, if any, clues to their regional identity. Their subject matter, of course, makes it obvious that they are writing about people, places and events in an area which is not Britain, the USA or some other country where the 'older' Englishes are spoken. However, from the text itself, the reader could not know whether the writer was a local speaker of a New English or, for example, an English writer who knew the region, its people and its customs well, as in this example from Singapore:

> She had been with the University for four years. She got on rather
> well both with staff and administration. Some women friends
> were scathing about her, and did not like the ease with which she
> moved among men.

Even the dialogue does not reflect any distinctive characteristics of Singapore English:

> She said, 'It's so hot, why not come in and have a drink?'
> 'Are you sure I shan't be disturbing you?' he asked.
> 'Not in the least, and the flat is airconditioned,' she replied
> without any hesitation.
> (Nalla Tan, 'Heat Wave', pp. 114, 119)

There are other writers, however, who clearly exhibit their regional identity by the variety of English used. Writers in areas where the New Englishes are spoken may, of course, write in English but translate the narrative and speech styles of another language. Kachru[1] mentions the 'predicament of a non-native creative writer in English' who has to reflect different styles and even stigmatized codes such as those used by members of the lower castes in India. However, a number of Indian writers have given an Indian flavour to the English they have used to represent the speech of characters who would actually speak some variety of an Indian language. He quotes an example from Lal Behari Day which, he suggests, 'is stylistically perhaps one of the first attempts toward nativizing English in "contact literature" in India':

> 'Come in,' said Badan, and jumped out of the verandah towards
> the door. 'Come in, Acharya Mahasaya; this is an auspicious day
> when the door of my house has been blessed with the dust of
> your honour's feet. Gayaram fetch an *asan* [a small carpet] for
> the Acharya Mahasaya to sit on.'
> (Lal Behari Day, *Govinda Samanta or History of a Bengal raiyat,* p. 48)

178

We shall consider first the way in which writers give a local quality to narrative and then the ways in which writers represent speech, both speech in a local variety of English and speech in another language spoken in the region.

The localization of English in narrative

There are several ways in which writers give a local quality to their narrative. This local quality in the narrative may be because the writer deliberately wishes to convey it, or because his English *is* a New English or because he translates from his local language into English. We cannot always tell the reason for this local quality and it is possible that sometimes two or more factors are working together.

A writer who is said to translate from his mother tongue into English is the Nigerian, Amos Tutuola. Evidently he has made a practice of writing in Yoruba and then translating into English.[2] The following passage is an example:

> When it was early in the morning of the next day, I had not palm-wine to drink at all, and throughout that day I felt not so happy as before; I was seriously sat down in my parlour, but when it was the third day that I had no palm-wine at all, all my friends did not come to my house again, they left me there alone, because there was no palm-wine for them to drink.
> (Amos Tutuola, *The Palm-Wine Drinkard*, p. 8)

Structures such as 'I felt not so happy as before', 'I was seriously sat down in my parlour' and 'all my friends did not come', although quite easily understood, give a very distinctive quality to the narrative.

Other writers write directly in English, but their narrative reflects the fact that English is not their native language. For example:

> They waited by the bus-stop and then alighted the STC bus together.
> (Goh Poh Seng, *If We Dream too Long*, p. 29)

where *alighted* is used instead of *boarded*.

Sometimes the narrative may reflect local English usage as in this example from a Malaysian Chinese writer:

> From the portal ceiling, the two Chinese lanterns, made of rice

paper and carrying the surname of the house in red letterings,
were taken down.
(Yeap Joo Kim, *The Patriarch*, p. 3)

where the plural marking of *letterings* shows the common reclassification of non-count nouns as count nouns discussed in Chapter 4.

Local critics are often quick to pounce on what they consider to be deviations from Standard English:

The book is full of 'Singaporeanese' — the 'isn't it?' question tag,
the dropping or adding of prepositions and a curious (sic!) usage
of verb tenses — which stamps it strongly as a local publication.
This is no criticism except that added to this, some meanings seem
to be confused or contradictory and blur the impact of the
language as an expressive tool — ' "Are you alright? Shall we go?"
were his *curt, polite* words' (p. 10). By definition 'curt' means
'short in manner; too short to be polite'. We have, therefore, a
contradiction in terms. And again 'Some had *instigated* him again'
(p. 82). We instigate something, not somebody. Neither do we
'impersonate a doctor's *role*'. 'One day I caught my fourteen-year
old hostel pupil on the act' (p. 168) is surely *in* the act.
(Doreen Rajaloo 'Review of G.J. Fernandez *Abode of Peace*[3])

In these works, the inclusion of features which mark the writing as belonging to a New English may not be deliberate. Sometimes, however, the use of words from local languages or the translation into English of local idioms and structures is deliberate. Attitudes towards these attempts to give a local flavour to the writing differ. For example, in Ghana, a favourable review of Abruquah's novel *The Catechist* mentions:[4]

no striving towards a hybrid of the English language that will pass
for African — a language which, almost alas! is becoming a tiresome
feature of so much West African fiction in English.

Of course, when a writer publishes locally and is aiming for a mainly local readership, the use of words from local languages and the use of expressions in the local New English may be greater. These words and expressions are meaningful to the local reader and they conjure up images in a way that non-local lexicon could not. For example, Philippine novelists writing in English often make use of Tagalog and Spanish expressions as in:

He got back his bolo from Nanay, slipped it into its sheath and hurried down the path to the *kaingin*. Tarang could see the tall dead trees of the clearing beyond the hinagdong tree and the second growth.
(N.V.M. Gonzalez *Children of the Ash-covered Loam and Other Stories*, p. 8)

It is interesting that the writer italicized *kaingin* but not 'bolo' and 'hinagdong' tree. Evidently he felt that *kaingin* was less integrated into the local English, although on p. 36 we find the word with the English plural suffix: *kaingins*. Also on p. 36 we find a device used by a number of authors, namely the use of a local word followed by its translation: 'that portion of the hut called the *sulambi* or sleeping place. . .'

Later (p. 43) we find the Spanish kinship terms *Tio* 'uncle' and *Tia* 'aunt' and the Spanish terms for garments:

Presently Lupo arrived with his father and mother —Lupo and his father Tio Longinos in a neat write *camisa de chinos*, and Tia Pulin in a dark starched-stiff cotton skirt and a hempen camisa.

This inclusion of non-English words and expressions reflects, although in a modified form, the use of mix-mix in the Philippines as mentioned in Chapter 10.

Stylistic influence from the local languages seems to be a particular feature of much Indian literature in English. For example,[5] 'to convey the "breathless" quality of the native Kannada narrative, Raja Rao resorts to endless coordination, the closest possible approximation of the chain of participial clauses that mark the Kannada narrative' as in this passage from *Kanthapura*:

Then the police inspector saunters up to the Skefflington gate, and he opens it and one coolie and two coolies and three coolies come out, their faces dark as mops, and their blue skin black under the clouded heavens, and perspiration flows down their bodies and their eyes seem fixed to the earth. . . .
(Raja Rao, *Kanthapura*, p. 137)

Beyond these reflections of local language structure is the translation of local idioms. Boadi[6] mentions that the verse of the Ghanaian poet George Kofi Awoonor contains Ewe idioms translated into English and refers to the 'deliberate cultivation of an "African idiom" . . . in the prose work of Christiana Aidoo.'

Such translations of words and idioms are common in Indian writing in English. Verma[7] mentions 'such idiosyncratic creations as *flowerbed, rape-sister, sister-sleeper*, and a host of similar expressions' and he goes on to say that 'they are not used even by their authors in their ordinary, everyday language. They are not deviations but arbitrary creations. They have been created in the process of finding translation equivalents of concepts and ideas deeply rooted in Indian writing. . . .'

It has been said of some Indian and African literature in English that it reflects a formal and even archaic style of English. This seems to be because of a combination of factors. Writing about West African literature, Young[8] says that:

> It is also possible that historical reasons can be found to account
> for the highly declamatory style also favoured by West African
> writers. This derives, in all probability from missionary influence.
> The main aim of the missionaries in teaching English was to make
> the Bible and the hymnal available to their new congregations.

Young feels, however, that the biblical flavour in West African writings has even deeper roots. In West African cultures, the language skill and the prestige of a person were related to his knowledge of traditional literature. Recitation of oral literature required a fairly highflown declamatory style. In this way, there was a similarity between the local style and the style of the Bible. This can be seen in an excerpt from a novel by D.O. Fagunwa:[8]

> When he said this, my soul was sweet, like the soul of a man in
> danger of prison who has been freed by the judge, because I had
> found what I had been seeking, and I had come across the thing
> I liked, and God had buttered my bread.

This combination of influences from English and local culture can also be seen in Indian writing. Das[9] states that 'Many Indians prefer poetic prose; this is perhaps because of such a tradition in our own literature. Figures of speech abound in the ordinary descriptive passages in Indian languages.' He also suggests that 'the teaching of English in schools and colleges has always been closely linked with the teaching of English literature' and that 'whatever little attention has been paid to the study of language has been mostly in the sphere of mechanical drill in grammar and a misguided induction of the learner into the secrets of idioms such as *to make both ends meet, to have too many irons in the fire, on the eve of, apple of discord*, etc.'

We have already mentioned in Chapter 6 the use of expressions which seem archaic in the older varieties of English. That they occur in literature and that narrative styles appear reminiscent of eighteenth- and nineteenth-century English literature is not surprising when we consider the combined influences of earlier English literary models and the literary styles of the background languages used in both oral and written literature.

The problem of dialogue

The representation of dialogue is a problem for the writer in those nations where the New Englishes are spoken. In fact, there are a number of problems. How does one represent other languages through the medium of English? In fact, how does one represent different social varieties and different styles of other languages through the medium of English? How does one represent the local varieties of English, the local creole or the local pidgin?

We shall first consider how some writers have attempted to represent other languages. There are three main methods:

1 to use a non-localized variety of English, with possibly the inclusion of some words and expressions from the language (s) which the characters would actually use;
2 to translate expressions and structures from local languages, again with the possible inclusion of words and expressions from these local languages;
3 to include dialogue in another language. This may be just sufficient to give authenticity, as the speaker would not, in real life, use English. If there is too much dialogue in another language, then there may be problems for those unfamiliar with the language.

The first method is used by writers from a number of countries. We have already seen its use by the Singaporean writer, Nalla Tan. Another example, but with the inclusion of Malay words, is from the short story 'Poonek':[10]

'Watch out, Mahsen, watch out!' Mahsen turned to look at Louisa. She was still sitting on the branch of the tree, but now she was pointing towards the water. '*Buaya*!' she screamed. 'A crocodile!' Mahsen looked at the river. The water was still. There was scarcely a ripple. . .

'No, no,' shouted Louisa, 'don't move that way. The crocodile
is on the other side of the bank. It is coming up the mud bank!'
(Lim Beng Hap, 'Poonek', p. 139)

Here the Malay word *buaya* is immediately translated by 'crocodile'.
Crewe comments[10] that 'the use of Standard English for the utterances of a simple village girl who is uneducated and unlikely even to
speak in the standard variety of Malay brings us back to the question
of stylistic variation.' He quotes another example of 'a conversation
which purports to take place between two coolies — the last utterance
in particular, both for its language and its sentiments belongs in the
mouth of an educated middle-class speaker and the whole dialogue
would be better replaced by a lively exchange in the Singapore L-
variety (Crewe is here referring to Colloquial Singapore English):

One day I met one of the old colleagues, by then working in
a provision store in Tanglin. He told me the rest. . . .
"What happend to our fat Madam and her children?" I asked.
"I don't know about the children," he replied, "but the fat
madam is working as a wash-amah for an army family in
Wessex Estate."
"I'm sorry to hear it," I said. "But it was entirely her own
fault. I only hope she realizes it now." '
(Tan Kok Seng, *Son of Singapore*, p. 79)

Of course, 'a lively exchange in the Singapore L- variety' may or
may not be understood by readers outside the region. We shall discuss
this later when looking at the use of local varieties of English for
dialogue.

The second method, translating expressions and structures from
local languages, again with the possible inclusion of some untranslated
words and expressions, is widely used:

I pray and pray to Allah every night. I visit the great banyan tree
beside the hot-water spring and pray and pray that our child, Allah
help her, could become well. But the ways of life are strange. I do
not understand it.
It is the will of Allah. If I am young and strong, it'll be all right.
But, you know we are not getting enough rice now, and I still owe
the rich ones five kunchas of rice.
(Lee Kok Liang, 'Just a Girl', p. 102[11])

Similarly, a Philippine writer has a peasant saying:

'Hey, Ricardo, son of Juan Suerte,' Gondoy shouted, 'don't you
hear the church bell in town ringing the Angelus? *Aba*, to look
at you one would think you married with a dozen children to feed.'
(Steven Javellana, *Without Seeing the Dawn*, p. 4)

In West Africa, many writers have their characters speaking in a type
of English which reflects the local language, for example Igbo:

I want one of my sons to join these people and be my eyes there.
If there is nothing in it you will come back. But if there is something there you will bring home my share. The world is like a
mask dancing.

Chinua Achebe[12] quotes this example from *Arrow of Gold* to exemplify
the importance of *form*: 'The Chief Priest is telling one of his sons why
it is necessary to send him to church.' Achebe continues:

Now supposing I had put it another way. Like this for instance:
    'I am sending you as my representative among these people —
    just to be on the safe side in case the new religion develops.
    One has to move with the times or one is left behind. I have
    a hunch that those who fail to come to terms with the white
    man may well regret their lack of foresight.'
The material is the same. But the form of the one is in character,
and the other is not. It is largely a matter of instinct but judgement
comes into it too.

Another Nigerian writer has the following dialogue between two
Fulani speakers of Northern Nigeria:

'A maiden is one of those things a man must not trust. By Allah,
it is!'
'And the others?'
'A prince, a river, a knife, and darkness.
A prince because his word changes with the weather; a river because
in the morning you may wade across it, but in the evening it has
swollen and can swallow you. A knife, because it knows not who
carries it. Darkness, ha! Who knows what lurks in it. Certainly,
all evil things.'
(Cyprian Ekwense, *Burning Grass*, p. 48)

This type of traditional wisdom seems very appropriate coming from the old man, Baba, the only person who has remained in the village after it has been evacuated because of a tsetse fly plague.

The reflection of local languages and their speech styles in English literature is a common feature in Indian English writing. Sridhar[5] gives examples from Raja Rao:

Questions without inversion:

'And you'll allow me to speak?'

'Brother, you are with me?'

'But I can hold meetings for you, Moorthy?'

Right and left dislocation (pronoun copying):

'My heart — it beat like a drum.'

'And he can sing too, can Jayaramachar.'

Mulk Raj Anand uses Hindi words in his novels, as in the following examples:[13]

'Don't do the *siapa* here' ('Seven Summers', p. 22)

'You have to keep the *ijjat* of the *paltan*' ('The Village', p. 208)

'*Sali*, she-ass, deceitful bitch' ('Private Life of an Indian Prince', p. 37)

'Who is this *buk-buk*?' ('Private Life of an Indian|Prince', p. 212)

Mehrotra[13] suggests that 'this may possibly be due to the fact that the Hindi words come more naturally and appear more forceful in a given context than their English equivalents. *Sister-in-law* is no match for *sali*, and *idle talk* is a poor substitute for *buk-buk*'. Unfortunately, however, such words may be meaningless to the reader outside India unless they are understood from the context or, as in our Malaysian example of *buaya* and 'crocodile', there is a translation.

The third method is probably less common as it is likely to make the work less accessible to an international public. However, skilfully used it can give considerable authenticity, especially in a play. It is a technique which has been successfully used in a number of BBC television series set in such countries as Greece and Spain. The British characters speak English. Local characters such as police inspectors use English in their dealings with them but the local language for short conversations with local people.

In Ngugi and Mugo's play *The Trial of Dedan Kimathi*, a mainly English-language play set in Kenya during the Mau Mau independence struggle in the 1950s, there are songs in kiSwahili and some of the dialogue is in it and in Kikuyu. Zuengler[14] points out that the play is set in a Kikuyu-speaking area but the songs are in kiSwahili because the language expresses 'concepts of unity and nationhood'. In the following excerpt, a dialogue between a white police officer and an African soldier, the use of kiSwahili gives an air of authenticity:

Waitina:	Askari!
(police officer)	
Second Soldier:	Fande!
Waitina:	Line up those Mau Mau villagers, two by two.
Second Soldier:	Tayari, Bwana!

However, the following dialogue between the main female character and a white soldier could be more difficult to understand unless the action made it intelligible (translations of the Pidgin Swahili are supplied here):

Woman:	Uuu-u! Nduri ici ni kii giki!
	(Kikuyu)
Johnnie:	Simama kabisa! Good. Passbook.
Woman:	Ati passi?
	(Is it a passbook)
Johnnie:	Ndiyo, passbook. Wapi passbook?
	(yes) (where is)

For his play *A Tiger is Loose in our Community*, the Malaysian playwright Edward Dorall suggests that:

Where Malay, Cantonese and Tamil are spoken in this play the actors concerned should feel free to use their own version based on the English rendering given.
(Edward Dorall, *A Tiger is Loose in our Community*)

In the play only utterances by minor characters are indicated as being in one of these languages, for example:

Hoong Tan:	I think you cheat ah.
San Fan	(*speaking in Cantonese as he slams down the cards*): Cheat ah? Say that again.
Hoong Tan	(*also in Cantonese*): You cheat.

Speech in the New Englishes

It is, of course, mainly in those nations where a New English is in daily use for spoken communication among a sizeable proportion of the population that writers can appropriately represent local varieties of English in their dialogues. That they do not always do so we have seen in the example from Tan earlier in this chapter. There may be several reasons for this:

1 The feeling that readers in other countries will have difficulty
   in understanding the dialogue. In reality, this is no problem if
   the dialogue is skilfully handled, as we shall see from some of
   the examples.

2 The feeling that it is wrong to use what they consider to be 'sub-
   standard' English even for characters who would, in real life, use it.
   Added to this is probably the fear that local critics, whether literary
   critics or those concerned with English language teaching, may
   condemn their use of stigmatized speech forms.

3 An inability to represent the various local forms of English
   appropriate to the particular character. Strange as it may seem,
   some highly educated speakers of the New Englishes are unable
   to analyze their own usage and the usage of those about them.
   This may be part of a linguistic insecurity that has been made all
   too prevalent by the branding of some of the local varieties of
   English as 'patois', 'pidgin' or 'creole', even when they are simply
   colloquial forms of the New Englishes.

In West Africa and the West Indies, it is, of course, true that the boundaries between the New English and the local pidgin or creole are not always clear. We shall therefore consider here the representation both of pidgins and creoles and of New Englishes in dialogues.

In the Kenyan play *The Trial of Dedan Kimathi* in which we saw how kiSwahili was used, Kimathi, one of the Mau Mau guerilla leaders, has a conversation with an Indian trader. As Zuengler points out,[14] 'both characters are speaking in a second language, but here the marked version is that of the Indian.' The speech of Kimathi, the idealist, is not marked by local features. The Indian, who is obviously portrayed as interested mainly in making money, speaks in what is almost a caricature of Indian English:

Indian: In India-a, ve got our independent. Preedom. To make
            money. This here, our true priend. Not racialism. Leaves
            your custom alone. You can pray Budha, pray Confucius,
            pray under the trees, pray rocks, vear sari. . .your culture
            . . .songs. . .dances. . .ve don't mind. . .propided. . .ve
            make money. . .priend. . .priend.

Kimathi: Some of our people passed through India on their way
            from Burma. Calcutta. Delhi. Bombay. They told of
            hungry peoples, beggars on pavements. . .wives selling
            themselves for a rupee. . .Have they now said 'no' to
            poverty?

Indian: Ve trying. Little. Little. But ve hawe our religion. Ve
            hawe our plag. Ve hawe national anthem. And now
            ewen Indian Bankers. Ha! Ha!

However, the representation of Indian English is not always for the
purpose of unfavourable contrast. The Singapore writer Catherine Lim,
in her short story 'A.P. Velloo'[15] has her kindly but pathetic old Tamil
Indian, a retired clerk who had worked for the British forces, speak and
write in a type of Indian English. He gives sweets and biscuits to the
neighbourhood children. One in particular, a little sub-normal girl,
often called on him. He has just read in the newspaper about 'Girl, 14,
Molested in Lift' and 'Girl Found Slain Behind School'. He decides to
write a letter to the Editor:

Dear Editor Sir,
    Everyday there is crimes in your newspaper. Young girls molested
in lifts and murder and rape and all sorts of evil things happening.
I should like to know is, What are police doing? What is Government
doing. How can allow murder and rape and all these things to go on.
Children they are innocent and precious and we adults must protect
them. . . . So I hope you will publish my letter in your esteemed
newspaper so all can know of the problem and how problem must be
solve by all faithful citizens.

                                    I remain
                                    Your Humble
                                    Servant
                                    A.P. Velloo

As his letter and a second letter are neither published nor acknow-
ledged he storms into the newspaper office, creates a scene and is

eventually dealt with by a 'cool, efficient-looking young man' who explains that not all letters are published unless found to be interesting and continues:

'And I'm sure yours is interesting Mr Velloo, but you'll have to be patient and wait a little.'

In reality, the young man would probably have spoken in a more distinctively Singaporean variety of English, especially to someone like Mr Velloo, but his utterance here is effective as it stands in marked contrast to A.P. Velloo's previous outburst:

'I want to see your Chief Editor!' yelled A.P. Velloo.
'I want to know why my letters not even one published. I want to ask your Chief whether he just throw my letters into the waste-paper basket! This is free, democratic country, let me tell you, sir! I, A.P. Velloo, have right to give my views! The Prime Minister got right, the Ministers got right, the Members of Parliament got right, A.P. Velloo got right too!'

Catherine Lim makes use of basilectal Singapore English in a number of short stories. In 'The Taximan's Story'[16] the whole story is a taxi driver's part (obviously the major part) of a dialogue with a woman passenger. He talks about young girls who associate with American and European tourists:

They usual is wait in bowling alley or coffee house or hotel and they walk up, and friend, friend, the European and American tourists and this is how they make fun and also extra money. Madam you believe or not when I tell you how much money they get?

The irony is that the taxi driver is furious and outraged when he finds his own school age daughter engaged in the same activities. The speech style of a Singapore taxi driver is well captured. How authentic this monologue is can be judged by comparison with the speech of a real Singapore taxi driver:[17]

Passenger depend lah — good one also got, bad one also got. Some ah some taxi driver they want to go to this tourist area like hotel ah. They park there, y'know. Then if the tourist want to go and buy things, buy anything ah, they book the taxi say one hour I pay you how much. Then after that they brought the passenger

go and buy thing already. Then the shop ah give commission to
the taxi driver lah. Don't know how many per cen.

In another Catherine Lim short story, 'The Teacher',[16] an unhappy
Secondary Four schoolgirl's composition upsets the teacher, who is
concerned mainly with 'correct' English:

> The teacher read, pausing at those parts which he wanted his
> colleague to take particular note of: ' "*My happiest day it is on that
> 12 July 1976 I will tell you of that happiest day. My father want
> me to help him in his cakes stall to sell cakes and earn money.
> He say I must leave school and stay home and help him. My
> younger brothers and sisters they are too young to work so they
> can go to school. My mother is too sick and weak as she just
> born a baby.*" Can anything be more atrocious than this? And
> she's going to sit for her General Certificate of Education in
> three months' time.'

Later compositions by the same girl upset him even more. When she
was supposed to write a story with the title 'The Stranger' she wrote
about her father:

> *He canned me everytime, even when I did not do wrong things
> still he canned me and he beat my mother and even if she sick,
> he wallops her.*

and the teacher comments:

> This composition is not only grossly ungrammatical but out of
> point. I had no alternative but to give her an F9 straightaway.
> God, I wish I could help her!

This is immediately followed by the final paragraph:

> When the news reached the school, the teacher was very upset and
> said, 'Poor girl. What? She actually jumped down from the eleventh
> floor? Such a shy, timid girl. If only she had told me of her
> problems. But she was always too shy and timid to speak up.'

The use of different sub-varieties of local English is effectively used
in Dorall's play *A Tiger is Loose in Our Community*, which we mentioned before as an example of a play in which other languages could be
used for some minor characters. One of the main characters in the
play, the young Eurasian, Philip, talks to his Chinese friend, Helen, in

the Lake Gardens in Kuala Lumpur. She has just playfully ruffled his hair and he has started to comb it:

Helen: I wish we come out like this every day. And do the same things.
Philip: Then I'll have to buy more brylcreem.
Helen: When you think they tell you?
Philip: Tell me what?
Helen: About the job. The advertising firm.
Philip: Oh that! I don't know. In a few days probably.
Helen: If you get it, then you go away.
Philip: I have to accept it first.
Helen: What you mean?
Philip: Well, I only went for interview because my father made me. I wasn't particularly interested.
Helen: But it's a good job. They send you to England for training, isn't it?

Helen's speech is more noticeably localized than Philip's but he does omit the indefinite article *an* before *interview*. Helen lives in a squatter settlement whereas Philip lives in a comfortable middle-class environment.

In Johnny Ong's novel *Run Tiger Run*, the main characters give little or no indication by their speech that they are Malaysians. However, some minor characters speak a kind of pidgin. An example is a young Indian boy, a *jaga kereta*:

'Ere, Mam, ere big place,' the skinny, shirtless Indian boy cried out loudly, panting for breath. He spoke in broken English.

She backed her car into the space now reserved for her by the twelve-year-old boy.

'Me jaga Mam car, yes?' the boy grinned, showing a set of stained, broken teeth. 'My friend no good.' He pointed a dirty finger to the other Indian boy standing a few feet away, a short, chubby, ten-year-old with Tarzan-long hair. 'He no good jaga. Very lazy. No speak Ingklis. No jaga. He play.'

She locked the car and told the Indian boy, 'Yes, you jaga Mam's car — Jaga good. No play, eh? Mam pay you twenty cents.'

Here, the young woman modifies her speech so that the boy will understand her.

The Nigerian writer Adaora Lily Ulasi depicts a court scene in a

Nigerian town in 1935. The British Assistant District Officer (ADO) is acting as magistrate. The court interpreter interprets:

'Mr Joseph Udochi. On July 26th a consignment of corrugated iron, the property of IOA Ltd, was found on your premises, covered with palm leaves. What do you say to that?'

'The ADO said, that you thief IOA zinc. What say?'

Joseph Udochi, a tall trader dressed in white drill shorts and blue shirt, carrying a bush helmet in his hand, went into a long-winded explanation.

'He said, he dumbfounded!'

'I dare say he is. Ask him whether the corrugated iron got there by osmosis.'

'He said, they come to your house by wind?'

The accused spread his hands, and added some further explanation.

'Mr Udochi said, Mr ADO, that he come back from work and he see it there.'

(Adaora Lily Udasi, *Many Things You No Understand*, p. 8)

Here, there is a very effective interplay between the ADO's fairly informal English and the interpreter's version in a variety of English which borders on Nigerian Pidgin.

In Chinua Achebe's novel *No Longer at Ease*, the author comments on one of the characters, a friend of the main character, Obi:

Whether Christopher spoke good or 'broken' English depended on what he was saying, where he was saying it, to whom and how he wanted to say it. Of course that was to some extent true of most educated people, especially on Saturday night. But Christopher was rather outstanding in thus coming to terms with a double heritage.

(pp. 109–10)

This is an interesting comment on the type of code-switching practised by Christopher, a graduate of the London School of Economics, who has just switched between 'Fine. What are you people doing this evening?' and 'Make we go dance somewhere?'

Later, when trying to park his car, Obi is 'directed by half a dozen half-clad little urchins who were standing around.
'Na me go look your car for you,' chorused three of them at once.

'O.K., Make you look am well,' said Obi to none in particular.

'Lock up your side,' he said quietly to Clara.

'I go look am well, sir,' said one of the boys stepping across Obi's path so that he would remark him well as the right person to receive a three-pence "dash" at the end of the dance.'

(p. 110)

These 'little urchins' obviously perform the same service in Lagos as the *jaga kereta* boys in Malaysia in Johnny Ong's novel.

At the dance, most of the dances were 'high-life' and the words of one of them, 'Gentleman Bobby' are given:

I was playing moi guitar *jeje*
A lady gave me a kiss.
Her husband didn't like it,
He had to drag him wife away.
Gentlemen, please hold your wife.
Father and mum, please hold your girls,
The calypso is so nice,
If they follow, don't blame Bobby.

(p. 111)

The words of the song help in conjuring up the atmosphere of the dance hall, noisy and smoke-filled.

In the Caribbean region, writers have represented different sub-varieties of speech ranging from creole to 'educated' English. As far back as 1914, H.G. de Lisser's novel *Jane's Career* represented different speech varieties: the creole of the servant girl Jane, who comes to Kingston from the country and of Sarah, another servant girl, and code switching between creole and Jamaican English by their employer, Mrs Mason and her daughter, Cynthia.[18]

The Trinidadian author Samuel Selvon reflects local speech in the dialogue, as in this exchange between Tiger, an Indian, and Joe, who is of African descent:

'Everything confused in my mind Joe, you know is a funny thing but I never grow up an Indian you know —'
'Well is bout three hundred time yuh tell me so already.'
(Samuel Selvon, *A Brighter Sun*, p. 195)[19]

Although the two are speaking in a creole-influenced English, their speech is represented in a way that creates no real problems for readers unfamiliar with the Trinidadian variety.

Our final example from the Caribbean region is also from Trinidad. V.S. Naipaul uses 'standard English' to represent speech in Hindi and he uses colloquial Trinidadian English as a direct representation of that speech variety. When a more standard variety of English is used by characters this is mentioned specifically[20] as in the following example:

'Ma said you beat her,' Savi said.
Mr Biswas laughed. 'She was only joking,' he said in English.
(*A House for Mr Biswas*, p. 194)

The daughter Savi is speaking in Hindi.

An example of Naipaul's representation of the local dialect is the following discussion between Ganesh (the first speaker) and his future father-in-law Ramlogan:[20]

'But you can't have nice wording on a thing like an invitation.'
'You is the educated man, sahib. You could think of some.'
'*R.S.V.P.*?'
'What that mean?'
'It don't mean nothing, but it nice to have.'
'Let we have it then sahib! You is a modern man, and too besides, it sound as pretty wording.'
(V.S. Naipaul, *The Mystic Masseur*, p. 49)

The dialogues in all these works are generally comprehensible to speakers of other varieties of English. The authors have been able to convey the flavour of local speech but have not sacrificed intelligibility for authenticity. A writer can, of course, represent even more localized, colloquial speech if he is willing to limit his target readership to those who can understand the local speech varieties. In the following example Mr Chan, a neighbour, talks to Mr Ho:

'Now they all (his mistress and "son") happy lah.
Already eat at Kentucky fried chicken and her dress $100 over, from Yaohan. . .show, they all see nice or not.'
'Wow!'
'The world is like that,' he philosophized. 'Earn money must spend. If not how can I be so generous? Twenty thousand dollars (profits from his shares) just come like that,' he snapped his fingers.
(Ho Khek Fong, 'PUB Bills', p. 18)

This short story makes highly effective use of colloquial Singapore English in the speech of the unscrupulous Mr Chan who, while objecting vehemently to any slight rent increase to cover rises in PUB (Public Utilities Board) bills is able to spend lavishly on his mistress.

An example of local writing where the narrative and the dialogue are in a highly localized variety of English is the typical Onitsha market story from southeastern Nigeria. Some characters may also be represented as speaking in Nigerian pidgin. For example, in *The Game of Love*, Chief Bombey uses pidgin to his daughter Agnes, a school teacher, who wants to marry Edwin, a clerk. Chief Bombey has arranged marriage with a doctor:

Agnes:	Good morning Papa.
Chief Bombey:	Good morning my picken, welcome.
Agnes:	Please papa, I have something to tell you and it is what brought me here today.
Chief Bombey:	Make you tell me if na money I go give you.
Agnes:	I am in love with one young man by name Edwin who is working as a senior clerk under U.A.C. Owerri. He promised to marry me and will be coming to see you on Sunday.
Chief Bombey:	Wethin you dey say my pickin? Who be that man? Wethin be love? You no go marriam. Now me be your father. I tell you say make you go teach love. Forget that man with all him love. Doctor hope go marry you. Na, you go be him second wife who go stay for him pleasure car with him always.

wethin 'what thing, what', *car* 'care'
(J. Abiakam *The Game of Love: A Classical Drama from West Africa*, pp. 41–2)

In another novel, General Hitler calls a meeting on 1 October 1913 (sic!). In answer to newsmen he says:

Hitler:	Germany have Army, Navy and Air Force of over 100,000,000 strong men and over 50,000,000 Police and in addition to this, all German citizens are trained to serve as soldiers.

Later, the newsmen ask:

Newsmen:	According to B.B.C., is it true that you don't believe in God?
Hitler:	No please, I strongly believe in God. B.B.C. is trying

> to mislead the world by saying that I have no belief in God.

In Britain, Wilson Church-hill (sic!) also has a news conference:

Newsmen: Is it true that King Judge is ill?
Church-hill: That is not the object of my news conference. However, the King is in a promising condition.

The story concludes with the trial of Hitler after the 1939–45 war. The final paragraph is an example of the narrative style:

> At this stage General Hitler broke the chains on his hands, jumped out of the dock and snatched a gun from one Interpol. He shot the gun up and down in the court. The court members including the judges took to their heels and ran for their lives. Then General Hitler disappeared, nobody could tell Hitler's whereabout up till today.

THE END

(J.C. Anorue, *The Complete Story and Trial of Adolf Hitler*, pp. 7, 10, and 36)

It is all too easy to sneer at this type of 'folk' literature. Whatever their literary worth, these works are of great interest as examples of the spread of and indigenization of English. They are proof that English has been used at the most popular and unsophisticated level. At the other end of the scale are works such as those of Chinua Achebe, V.S. Naipaul and Catherine Lim, which can be read and appreciated for their literary worth, not only in the areas where they were written but throughout the English-speaking world. They are further proof that English belongs to all who use it.

CHAPTER 12

What will happen to the New Englishes?

All living languages and language varieties are constantly changing in form and function. This, of course, is happening with the New Englishes which we have been discussing in this book. Some will develop further, fulfilling more and more functions. For others, their range of functions may diminish and they may gradually become less like a New English and, for a large sector of the community, more like a foreign language. How a New English develops will, to a great extent, depend on government language policies in general and on educational policies in particular. It will also depend on the attitudes which the people in the New Nation have to particular policies.

It seems unrealistic to imagine a country where English shared absolutely *equal* rights or functions with a local language or a local lingua franca. Even if this were official policy, in reality one language or the other would take over the more official functions and would therefore eventually gain higher status.

This leaves three main possibilities:

(1) A local language as national and/or official language.
     No functions or very limited functions for English.
(2) A local language as national and/or official language.
     Some, often quite important, functions for English.
(3) English as national and/or official language, usually with a wide
     range of functions. Some functions for the local languages.

The term *official and/or national language* as it is used here does not necessarily mean by *government decree* but rather 'a language which has the functions of a national/official language'.

The term *local language* would also need to include a local lingua franca, a wider language of communication, such as Swahili in East Africa.

There are, of course, variations on these three main approaches. For example, in Singapore, in addition to English, Mandarin – which is not a local language – is favoured by the government rather than the dominant local Chinese dialect Hokkien. Singapore also considers Malay and Tamil as official languages.

Consistent policies using an approach outlined under (3) would be more likely to bring about a fully developed, highly functional New English. Policies outlined under (1), on the other hand, may result in the 'death' of the New English. English would remain only as a series of learners' interlanguages.[1]

A nation which has adopted policies outlined under (1) is Malaysia. Before Bahasa Malaysia (Malay) became the national language, a strongly developing variety of a New English, Malaysian English, existed[2] which was practically identical to Singapore English. The conversion process from English to Bahasa Malaysia throughout the education system is now complete. Already the range of functions for English has diminished and the type of English used has changed considerably, particularly among speakers of the younger generation. Although there has lately been some concern in government circles about the 'decline of English', it appears doubtful whether language policies will be drastically changed and, in the words of educated Malaysians[3] 'It is predicted that in years to come English will in reality assume the role of a foreign language in Malaysia. . .' The same may happen in Tanzania, where kiSwahili has replaced English not only as a medium of instruction but also as one of the functional varieties.

Two countries where there has been a reversal in language policies are Burma and Sri Lanka. In 1981, it was reported[4] that President U Ne Win had instituted a crash programme for the reintroduction of English in Burma. Recently, English has been reinstated as a subject in primary schools and it will again be the medium of instruction for several subjects at Rangoon University.[5] This is only a modest beginning and still within the scope of approach (1) but it is certainly worth watching.

The other country where English has been replaced as official language by a local language is Sri Lanka. For some time, the functions of English were certainly very restricted. However, President Junius Jayewardene recently announced[5] 'that English would be made a national language to ease communication between local communities and the rest of the world.' It would share its status as a national language with Tamil. As 'national languages may be used to conduct official functions', this decision of the President may help to increase the range of functions of English in Sri Lanka.

Three countries which appear to have followed policies outlined under (2) are Kenya, Uganda and the Philippines. Kenya and Uganda have opted for kiSwahili as national language and the Philippines have chosen Pilipino (Tagalog) as national language. It appears, according to the opinions of educated speakers from these countries, that English still has important functions. But they agree that this is more so in the towns and capital cities than in the rural areas. It appears that whatever the future trends will be, English will be widely used by an educated elite but that its functions may even decrease for the rest of the community, particularly in rural areas. This is expressed by Gonzales for the Philippines.[6] He was asked:

Can English stay strong in spite of the spread of Pilipino?

and his answer was:

At the popular level the future of English isn't very bright.
Based on our projections, by the year 2000 every Filipino will
be able to speak at least conversational Pilipino. This is a desirable
trend. The only unhappy result I foresee is that of a dichotomy in
the population — we will have a mass of people who probably will
not have a mastery of English beyond the comprehension level
and another elite group who will continue to use the language
here and abroad.

Among the countries which have adopted an approach of the type outlined under (3) are Ghana, Nigeria, Zambia and Singapore. We have already mentioned that Singapore may be regarded as a rather special case.

In the three African nations, English is used as the medium of instruction and for many functions in the community. It often enjoys a high status as against the local languages. But this does not necessarily meet with the approval of all. Although the importance of English is recognized, there have been moves not only to have local languages used for instruction in the early years of primary school but also to extend their range as school subjects and subjects at colleges and universities.[7] These efforts to revive an interest and pride in the local languages are naturally to be applauded. However, we do not think that in the near future this revival will affect the range of functions and the development of the New English in these nations.

Singapore English is probably one of the most developed of all the New Englishes. It has a range of social varieties and stylistic alternatives. There even appear to be interesting beginnings of the development of a 'more educated' colloquial form — and creative writers in the republic are beginning to explore the potential of the local English.

Whatever the dictates of language policies, there are two reasons why English is needed in the New Nations. One is its use as an international language all over the world and the other is its use as a neutral lingua franca, a neutral language of wider communication without a country.[8] The first need could be fulfilled by a small English-educated elite but the other one could not. In nations where there is a great ethnic and language diversity and where no alternative lingua franca exists, English may be required for some time to come. This can be seen from comments made about language situations in countries such as Nigeria and Fiji, e.g. Nigeria:[9]

> The multi-ethnic situation in Nigeria, and the accompanying
> emotional attachment to ethnic identity by various groups,
> required the adoption of a neutral language.

Fiji:[10]

> Multilingual nations such as Fiji, which lack a contending national
> lingua franca, give English a clearer path to second-language status.
> The neutral role of English in such situations. . .is political in
> character, i.e. giving no group the advantage of having its own
> language singled out for official status.

Is it worthwhile, useful or even desirable to talk of an Indian English, Singapore English, Nigerian English, etc.? We think it is. A New English can provide a background and an identity for its speakers which an 'alien' English, 'something from abroad', never could. And looking at it quite realistically, if some of them exist, as they obviously do, and are used by a large number of people, why not give them a name?

Appendix: Some phonetic symbols

Some phonetic symbols which are used in this book and which may be unfamiliar to the reader.

All the examples are from educated Southeastern British English.

$[\theta]$ the sound at the beginning of *thick*
$[\eth]$ the sound at the beginning of *they*
$[z]$ the sound at the end of *bees*
$[\iota]$ the vowel sound in *pit*
$[\epsilon]$ the vowel sound in *bed*
$[\ni]$ the second vowel sound in *mother*
$[æ]$ the vowel sound in *hat*
$[a]$ the vowel sound in *fast*
$[\ni]$ the vowel sound in *port*
$[\upsilon]$ the vowel sound in *put*
$[:]$ after a vowel means length, e.g. [fɑːst]

Notes

Further details of books and articles referred to are given in the Bibliography. If no page references are given, we are referring to the whole article.

Chapter 1 New Englishes and New Nations

1 Strevens, 1981, p.2.
2 Kachru, 1981, pp. 17–18.
3 Sey, 1973, p. 148.
4 Brosnahan, 1959, p. 98.
5 Jibril, 1982, p. 75.
6 Wells, 1982, p. 578.
7 Jibril, 1982, p. 75.
8 Strevens, 1982, p. 25.
9 Shnukal, 1982, pp. 24–5, also Angogo and Hancock, 1980, p. 72.
10 Bickerton, 1975, p. 24.
11 Angogo and Hancock, 1980, p. 72.

Chapter 2 The role of English

1 Moag, 1982a, p. 275.
2 Akere, 1982, p. 89.
3 Todd, 1982b, p. 123, also Jibril, 1982, p. 74 and Serpell, 1982, p. 103.
4 Shnukal, 1982, p. 26.
5 Todd 1982a, p. 284, also Jibril, 1982, p. 73.
6 Shnukal, 1982, p. 31, also Todd, 1982b, p. 131.
7 Todd 1982b, p. 136.
8 Allan, 1979.

9 Jibril, 1982, p. 74.
10 Olutoye, 1983, p. 1.
11 Serpell, 1982, p. 101.
12 Lawton, 1982, p. 268.
13 Parasher, 1979, p. 72.
14 Mehrotra, 1977, p. 165.
15 Parasher, 1979, p. 69.
16 Fernando, 1977, p. 345.
17 Kaplan, 1982, p. 2.
18 Gonzalez, 1980, p. 157.
19 Fishman, 1982, p. 17.
20 Platt and Weber, 1980, p. 161, also Wong and Ee, 1975, pp. 107-12.
21 Platt and Weber, 1982, pp. 73-9.
22 Luke and Richards, 1982, pp. 48-9.
23 Platt, 1982, p. 407.
24 Taylor, 1982, p. 10.
25 Moag and Moag, 1977, pp. 9-10.
26 Taylor, 1982, pp. 11-12.
27 Kaplan, 1982, p. 2.
28 Kachru 1982a, p. 356.
29 Platt and Weber, 1980, p. 119.
30 Scotton and Ury, 1977, p. 7, also Zuengler, 1982, p. 114.

Chapter 3 New accents

1 Smith, 1978, p. 28.
2 Sey, 1973, p. 150.
3 Hill, 1973, p. 5.
4 Wells, 1982, pp. 636ff.
5 Angogo and Hancock, 1980, p. 74.
6 Wells, 1982, pp. 560-72.
7 Hancock and Angogo, 1982, p. 314.
8 Todd, 1982a, p. 287.
9 Jibril, 1982, p. 76.
10 Sethi, 1981, p. 2, also Bansal, 1978.
11 Kandiah, 1981, p. 64.
12 Fernando, 1977, p. 348.
13 Bansal, 1978, p. 2.
14 Hancock and Angogo, 1982, p. 313.
15 Wells, 1982, p. 569.
16 Sey, 1973, p. 153, also Adejare and Afolayan, 1982, p. 8.
17 Bansal, 1969, p. 13.
18 Wells, 1982, p. 584.

19 Hancock and Angogo, 1982, p. 113, also Wells, 1982, p. 640.
20 Bansal, 1978.
21 Llamzon, 1969.
22 Wells, 1982, pp. 570ff.
23 Sethi, 1981, p. 5.
24 Hancock and Angogo, 1982, p. 313.
25 Wells, 1982, p. 580.
26 Sey, 1973, p. 15.
27 Platt and Weber, 1980, pp. 49-52.
28 Wells, on a cassette accompanying Wells, 1982.

Chapter 4 One or more and other problems

1 Platt, Weber and Ho, 1983a.
2 Craig, 1982, p. 202.
3 Ho, 1981, p. 71.
4 Smith, 1978, pp. 34ff.
5 Kirk-Greene, 1971, p. 134.
6 Gonzalez, 1983, p. 167.
7 Sey, 1973, p. 28.
8 Bashir Ikara, 1981, p. 5, also Jibril, 1982, p. 78.
9 Hancock and Angogo, 1982, p. 316.
10 Adapted from Bickerton, 1981, pp. 147ff.
11 Adapted from Bickerton, 1981, pp. 23ff.
12 Spitzbardt, 1976, p. 40.
13 Smith, 1978, p. 40.
14 Platt, 1982, p. 410.
15 Quirk et al., 1972.
16 Sey, 1973, p. 30, also Tingley, 1981, p. 43.
17 Sey, 1973, p. 32.
18 Quirk, et al., 1972.
19 Smith, 1978, p. 19.
20 Tingley, 1981, p. 57.
21 Kirk-Greene, 1971, p. 136.
22 Kirk-Greene, 1971, p. 134, also Jibril, 1982, p. 79.

Chapter 5 Actions, states and perceptions

1 Hinnebusch, 1979, p. 214.
2 Gonzalez, 1983, p. 163, also Bautista, 1981, p. 8.
3 Platt, 1977a, p. 28.
4 Kirk-Greene, 1971, p. 135.
5 Jibril, 1982, p. 79.
6 Bautista, 1981, p. 8.
7 Verma, 1982, p. 182.
8 Gonzalez, 1983, p. 162.

9   Carr, 1972, p. 150.
10 Kachru, 1982a, p. 360.
11 Smith, 1978, p. 21.
12 Sey, 1973, pp. 34–5.
13 Angogo and Hancock, 1980, p. 76.
14 Crewe, 1977b, p. 50.
15 Gonzalez, 1983, p. 166.
16 Platt, 1977b, p. 77.
17 Platt, 1983b.
18 Carr, 1972, p. 139.
19 Carr, 1972, p. 131.
20 Quirk et al., 1972.
21 Hancock and Angogo, 1982, p. 316.
22 Tingley, 1981, pp. 48–9.
23 Crewe, 1977b, p. 56 and pp. 58–9.
24 Carr, 1972, p. 153.
25 Bamgbose, 1982, p. 106, also Sey, 1973, p. 55.
26 Tay and Gupta, 1981, p. 29.
27 Tingley, 1981, also Sey, 1973, p. 51 and Bamgbose, 1982, p. 106.
28 Carr, 1972, pp. 132 and 142.
29 Kirk-Greene, 1971, p. 140, also Tingley, 1981, p. 49.
30 Some of these reasons have also been suggested by Sey, 1973.

Chapter 6 New words and new meanings

1   Jibril, 1982, p. 81.
2   Todd, 1982a, p. 288.
3   Gonzalez, 1983, p. 156.
4   Bautista, 1981, p. 15.
5   Carr, 1972, p. 120.
6   Kachru, 1982a, pp. 361–3.
7   LePage and Cassidy, 1967, p. 164.
8   Smith, 1981, pp. 13–15, also supplied by educated speakers of
        Papua New Guinean English.
9   Verma, 1982, p. 180.
10 Kirk-Greene, 1971, pp. 138 and 140.
11 Mehrotra, 1982, p. 160.
12 Sey, 1973, pp. 80–1.
13 Hancock and Angogo, 1982, p. 317.
14 Bashir Ikara, 1981, pp. 7–8, also Bokamba, 1982, p. 89, Bamgbose,
        1982, pp. 106–7, Jibril, 1982, pp. 81–2 and Sey, 1973, pp. 76–8.
15 Kandiah, 1981, pp. 64–5.
16 Gonzalez, 1983, pp. 158–9.
17 Carr, 1972, pp. 120–58.
18 LePage and Cassidy, 1967, p. 189.
19 Bamgbose, 1982, p. 106.
20 Bamgbose, 1971, pp. 43–4.

21 Adejare and Afolayan, 1982.
22 Ajulo, 1982, p. 16, also Akere, 1982, pp. 90–1, and Sey, 1973,
    p. 119.
23 Tongue, 1979, pp. 87–8.
24 Craig, 1982, p. 202.
25 Leong, 1978, p. 312.
26 Platt and Ho, 1982, p. 269.
27 Bashir Ikara, 1981, p. 8, also Angogo and Hancock, 1980, p. 77.
28 Platt, Weber and Ho, 1983b.
29 Cassidy, 1971, pp. 71–2.

Chapter 7 New ways of saying it

1   Angogo and Hancock, 1980, pp. 75–6.
2   Smith, 1978, pp. 23–5 and 31–4.
3   Bakamba, 1982, pp. 83–6.
4   Kandiah, 1981, p. 70.
5   Gonzalez, 1983, pp. 161–2.
6   Carr, 1972, pp. 121 and 158.
7   Adapted from Platt and Weber, 1980, p. 79.
8   Kachru, 1982a, pp. 360 and 374.
9   Verma, 1982, p. 181.
10 Quirk et al., 1972.
11 Todd, 1982a, p. 289.
12 Adapted from Platt and Weber, 1980, pp. 74–6.
13 Tongue, 1979, p. 48.

Chapter 8 New tunes on an old language

1   Platt and Weber, 1980, pp. 55–6.
2   Sethi, 1981, p. 7.
3   Bansal, 1978, pp. 5–7.
4   Adejare and Afolayan, 1981, p. 8.
5   Mafeni, 1971, pp. 108–9.
6   Abercrombie, 1965.
7   Richards, Platt and Weber, forthcoming.
8   Todd, 1982a, p. 288, and Bamgbose, 1982, p. 42.
9   Lawton, 1982, p. 257.
10 Luke and Richards, 1982, p. 60.
11 Tay, 1982, p. 139, also Platt and Weber, 1980, p. 57.
12 Carr, 1972, pp. 44 and 50–1.
13 Bansal, 1978, pp. 5–6.
14 Ohala, 1977, p. 327 quoted by Nelson, 1982, p. 68.
15 Brazil, Coulthard and Johns, 1980, pp. 15–22.
16 The term RP (Received Pronunciation) has been used for the accent
    of educated English upper and upper-middle class speakers.

17 The speakers are on the cassette accompanying Trudgill and
        Hannah, 1982.
18 Bautista, 1981, p. 12.

Chapter 9 Styles and strategies

1 Platt and Weber, 1980, pp. 111-16, also Platt, 1983a.
2 Craig, 1982, p. 198.
3 Minderhout, 1977.
4 Bickerton, 1975, p. 187.
5 Lawton, 1980.
6 Gumperz, 1978, quoted in Richards, 1982, p. 239.
7 Gonzalez, 1982, p. 213.
8 Richards, 1982, p. 240.
9 Mehrotra, 1982, pp. 162-66.
10 Chishimba, 1980 (a) and (b), quoted by Kachru, 1982c, p. 338.
11 Kachru, 1982c, pp. 337-8.
12 Sey, 1973, p. 95.
13 Subrahmanian, 1978, p. 296.
14 Hymes, 1974, pp. 45-65.
15 Carr, 1972, p. 124.
16 Akere, 1982, p. 96.
17 Fernando, 1977, p. 349.
18 Jibril, 1982, p. 81.
19 Angogo and Hancock, 1980, p. 77.
20 Kachru, 1982a, p. 374.
21 Bokamba, 1982, pp. 84-5.
22 Kirk-Greene, 1971, pp. 133-7.
23 Tongue, 1979, p. 85.

Chapter 10 The teacher's dilemma

1 Prator, 1968, p. 459.
2 Kachru, 1979, pp. 8-9 and 13.
3 Kachru, 1982d, p. 41, makes a similar division.
4 Boadi, 1971, pp. 53-4.
5 Platt and Weber, 1980, pp. 112ff.
6 Bamgbose, 1982, pp. 99 and 105.
7 Hocking, 1974, pp. 57-8, quoted by Angogo and Hancock, 1980,
        p. 79.
8 Tay, 1979, pp. 107-8.
9 Boadi, 1971, p. 53.
10 Akere, 1982, pp. 87-8.
11 Kandiah, 1981, p. 68.
12 RELC Country Workshop Report: Philippines, 1981.
13 Lee Sow Ling, 1981, p. 7.

14 Tay and Gupta, 1981, p. 4.
15 Strevens, 1980, pp. 87–8.
16 Moag, 1982b, p. 32.
17 Sey, 1973, p. 7.
18 Tongue, 1979, Introduction.
19 Adapted from Haynes, 1982, p. 212.
20 Adapted from Kachru, 1979, p. 8.
21 Platt and Weber, 1980, p. 184.
22 Bansal, 1969, quoted in Kachru, 1979, p. 9.
23 Mehrotra, 1982, p. 169.
24 Nelson, 1982, p. 169.
25 Halliday, 1978.
26 Gumperz and Roberts, 1980, p. 1.
27 Foley, 1982, p. 6.

Chapter 11 The writer and the New Englishes

1 Kachru, 1982c, p. 342.
2 Young, 1971, p. 172.
3 Quoted and discussed by Crewe, 1978, p. 81.
4 Joe de Graft in *Okyeame*, 3/1, 1966, quoted by Boadi, 1971, p. 64.
5 Sridhar, 1982, p. 297.
6 Boadi, 1971, p. 63.
7 Verma, 1982, p. 177.
8 Young, 1971, pp. 175–6.
9 Das, 1982, p. 143.
10 Crewe, 1978, pp. 83–4.
11 Yap, 1976, p. 69.
12 Achebe, 1965, p. 29, quoted by Sridhar, 1982, p. 299.
13 Mehrotra, 1982, pp. 161–2.
14 Zuengler, 1982, pp. 119–22.
15 In Lim, 1980, pp. 22–38.
16 In Lim, 1978, pp. 13–15 and pp. 76–9.
17 Taken with modified spelling from Platt, Weber and Ho, 1983a.
18 Lawton, 1980, pp. 217–20.
19 Ramchand, 1976, p. 59.
20 Weir, 1982, pp. 315–16.

Chapter 12 What will happen to the New Englishes?

1 Selinker, 1972.
2 Platt, 1976.
3 RELC Country Workshop Report: Malaysia, 1981, p. 2.
4 Kaplan, 1982, p. 1.
5 *Singapore Bulletin*, March 1983, p. 11.

6 In an interview with Gonzalez, *Asiaweek*, February 25, 1983, p. 54.
7 Olutoye, 1983.
8 Pride, 1979, pp. 34ff.
9 Akere, 1982, p. 89.
10 Moag, 1982a, p. 275.

Bibliography

Abercrombie, D., 1965, *Studies in Phonetics and Linguistics*, London: Oxford University Press.

Abiakam, J. (n.d.), *The Game of Love: A Classical Drama from West Africa*, Onitsha, Nigeria: J.C. Brothers Bookshop.

Achebe, C., 1960, *No Longer at Ease*, London and Ibadan: Heinemann.

Achebe, C., 1965, English and the African Writer, *Transition*, 4/18, 27–30.

Adejare, O. and Afolayan, A., 1982, Semiotics: the unexplored level of variation in second language use. Paper presented at 17th Regional Seminar, SEAMEO Regional Language Centre, Singapore.

Adetugbo, A., 1977, Nigerian English: fact or fiction? *Lagos Notes and Records*, 6, 128–41.

Ajulo, E.B., 1982, Sociocultural influences on the English of second language users. Paper presented at 17th Regional Seminar, SEAMEO Regional Language Centre, Singapore.

Akere, F., 1982, Sociocultural constraints and the emergence of a Standard Nigerian English, in J. Pride (ed.), *New Englishes*.

Allan, K., 1979, Nation, tribalism and national language: Nigeria's case, in *Cahiers d'Etudes africaines*, 71/XVIII-3, 397–415.

Angogo, R. and Hancock, I., 1980, English in Africa, *English World-Wide*, 1/1, 67–96.

Anorue, J.C. (n.d.), *The Complete Story and Trial of Adolf Hitler*, Onitsha, Nigeria: J.C. Brothers Bookshop.

Bailey, R.W. and Görlach, M. (eds), 1982, *English as a World Language*, Ann Arbor: University of Michigan Press.

Bamgbose, A., 1971, The English language in Nigeria, in J. Spencer (ed.), *The English language in West Africa*.

Bamgbose, A., 1982, Standard Nigerian English: issues of identification, in B.B. Kachru (ed.), *The Other Tongue: English across Cultures*.

211

Bansal, R.K., 1969, *The Intelligibility of Indian English*, Monograph 4, Hyderabad: Central Institute of English.

Bansal, R.K., 1978, Phonetic research relevant to English language teaching in India. Paper presented at 13th Regional Seminar, SEAMEO Regional Language Centre, Singapore.

Bashir Ikara, 1981, Some linguistic and sociocultural variables in a Nigerian Variety of English. Paper presented at 16th Regional Seminar, SEAMEO Regional Language Centre, Singapore.

Bautista, M.L.S., 1981, Yaya English: an idiosyncratic dialect of Philippine English. Paper presented at 16th Regional Seminar, SEAMEO Regional Language Centre, Singapore.

Bickerton, D., 1975, *Dynamics of a Creole System*, Cambridge: Cambridge University Press.

Bickerton, D., 1981, *Roots of Language*, Ann Arbor: Karoma Publishers.

Boadi, L.A. 1971, Education and the role of English in Ghana, in J. Spencer (ed.), *The English Language in West Africa*.

Bokamba, E.G., 1982, The Africanization of English, in B.B. Kachru (ed.), *The Other Tongue: English across Cultures*.

Brazil, D.C., Coulthard, M. and Johns, C., 1980, *Discourse Intonation and Language Teaching*, London: Longman.

Brosnahan, L.F., 1959, English in Southern Nigeria, *English Studies*, 39/3, 91–110.

Carr, E.B., 1972, *Da kine talk. From Pidgin to Standard English in Hawaii*, Honolulu: University Press at Hawaii.

Cassidy, F.G., 1971, *Jamaica Talk*, London: Macmillan.

Chishimba, M.M., 1980a, The English language in the sociolinguistic profile of Zambia: the educational aspects. Unpublished manuscript.

Chishimba, M.M., 1980b, Some bilingual and bicultural aspects of African creative writing. Unpublished manuscript.

Craig, D.R., 1982, Toward a description of Caribbean English, in B.B. Kachru (ed.), *The Other Tongue: English across Cultures*.

Crewe, W.J., 1977a, *The English Language in Singapore*, Singapore: Eastern Universities Press.

Crewe, W.J., 1977b, *Singapore English and Standard English*, Singapore: Eastern Universities Press.

Crewe, W.J., 1978, The Singapore writer and the English language, *RELC Journal*, 9/1, 77–86.

Das, S.K., 1982, Indian English, in J. Pride (ed.), *New Englishes*.

Day, L.B., 1874, *Govinda Samanta or History of a Bengal Raiyat*, London: Macmillan, 2 vols (reprinted 1878 under the title *Bengal Peasant Life*).

Dorall, E., 1972, *A Tiger is Loose in Our Community*, in L. Fernando (ed.), *New Drama One*.

Ekwensi, C., 1962, *Burning Grass*, London and Ibadan: Heinemann.

Fernando, C., 1977, English and Sinhala bilingualism in Sri Lanka, *Language in Society*, 6/3, 341–60.

Fernando, L., 1968, *Twenty-two Malaysian Stories*, Kuala Lumpur: Heinemann.

Fernando, L., 1972, *New Drama One*, Kuala Lumpur: Oxford University Press.

Fishman, J.A., 1982, Sociology of English as an additional language, in B.B. Kachru (ed.), *The Other Tongue: English across Cultures*.

Foley, J.A., 1982, Some thoughts on psycholinguistic processes underlying linguistic transfer. Paper presented at 17th Regional Seminar, SEAMEO Regional Language Centre, Singapore.

Goh, P.S., 1972, *If We Dream too Long*, Singapore: Island Press.

Gonzalez, A.B. FSC., 1980, *Language and Nationalism: The Philippine Experience thus far*, Manila: Ateneo de Manila University Press.

Gonzalez, A.B. FSC., 1982, English in the Philippines, in J. Pride (ed.), *New Englishes*.

Gonzalez, A.B. FSC., 1983, When does an error become a feature of Philippine English? in R.B. Noss (ed.), *Varieties of English in Southeast Asia*.

Gonzalez, N.V.M., 1977, *Children of the Ash-Covered Loam and Other Stories*, Manila: Bookmark.

Gumperz, J.J., 1978, The sociolinguistic significance of conversational code switching, *RELC Journal*, 8, 1–34.

Gumperz, J.J. and Roberts, C., 1980, *Developing Awareness Skills for Interethnic Communication*. Occasional Papers No. 12 Singapore: SEAMEO Regional Language Centre.

Halliday, M.A.K., 1978, *Language as Social Semiotic*, London: Edward Arnold.

Hancock, I.F. and Angogo, R., 1982, English in East Africa, in R.W. Bailey and M. Görlach (eds), *English as a World Language*.

Haynes, L.M., 1982, Caribbean English: form and function, in B.B. Kachru (ed.), *The Other Tongue: English across Cultures*.

Hill, T., 1973, The pronunciation of English stressed vowels in Tanzania, *Bulletin of the Language Association of Tanzania*, 4/2, 4–13.

Hinnebusch, T.J., 1979, Swahili, in T. Shopin (ed.), *Languages and Their Status*, Cambridge, Mass.: Winthrop Publishers.

Ho, K.F., 1981, PUB Bills, *Singa: Literature and the Arts in Singapore*, 3, 16–18.

Ho, M.L., 1981, The noun phrase in Singapore English. Unpublished M.A. thesis, Monash University, Australia.

Hocking, B.D.W., 1974, *All what I was Taught and Other Mistakes*, Nairobi: Oxford University Press.

Hymes, D., 1974, *Foundations in Sociolinguistics, An Ethnographic Approach*, Philadelphia: University of Pennsylvania Press.

Javellana, S., 1976, *Without Seeing the Dawn*, Quezon City, Philippines: Alemar-Phoenix Publishing House.

Jibril, M., 1982, Nigerian English: an introduction, in J.B. Pride (ed.), *New Englishes*.

Kachru, B.B., 1979, Models of English for the third world: white man's linguistic burden or language pragmatics, in J.C. Richards (ed.),

New Varieties of English: Issues and Approaches (Reprinted from *TESOL Quarterly*, 1976, 10/2.)

Kachru, B.B., 1981, The pragmatics of non-native varieties of English, in L.E. Smith (ed.), *English for Cross-cultural Communication*.

Kachru, B.B., 1982a, South Asian English, in R.W. Bailey and M. Görlach (eds), *English as a World Language*.

Kachru, B.B. 1982b, *The Other Tongue: English across Cultures*, Urbana: University of Illinois Press.

Kachru, B.B. 1982c, Meaning in deviation: toward understanding non-native English texts, in B.B. Kachru (ed.), *The Other Tongue: English across Cultures*.

Kachru, B.B., 1982d, Models for non-native Englishes, in B.B. Kachru (ed.), *The Other Tongue: English across Cultures*.

Kandiah, T., 1981, Lankan English schizoglossia, *English World-Wide*, 2/1, 63–81.

Kaplan, R.B., 1982, The language situation in the Philippines, *The Linguistic Reporter*, 24/5, 1–4.

Kirk-Greene, A., 1971, The influence of West African languages on English, in J. Spencer (ed.), *The English Language in West Africa*.

Lawton, D., 1980, Language attitude, discreteness and code shifting in Jamaican Creole, *English World-Wide*, 1/2, 211–26.

Lawton, D., 1982, English in the Caribbean, in R.W. Bailey and M. Görlach (eds), *English as a World Language*.

Lee, K.L. 1968, Just a girl, in L. Fernando (ed.), *Twenty-one Malaysian Stories*.

Lee, S.L., 1981, English language indigenization and planning in Singapore. Paper presented at the 16th Regional Seminar, SEAMEO Regional Language Centre, Singapore.

Leong, C.C., 1978, *Youth in the Army*, Singapore: Federal Publications.

LePage, R.B. and Cassidy, F.G. 1967, *Dictionary of Jamaican English*, Cambridge: Cambridge University Press.

Lim, B.H., 1968, Poonek, in L. Fernando (ed.), *Twenty-one Malaysian Stories*.

Lim, C., 1978, *Little Ironies – Stories of Singapore*, Singapore: Heinemann.

Lim, C., 1980, *Or Else the Lightning God and Other Stories*, Singapore: Heinemann.

Llamzon, T.A., 1969, *Standard Filipino English*, Manila: Ateneo University Press.

Luke, K.K. and Richards, J.C., 1982, English in Hong Kong: functions and status, *English World-Wide*, 3/1, 47–64.

Mafeni, B., 1971, Nigerian Pidgin, in J. Spencer (ed.), *The English Language in West Africa*.

Mehrotra, R.R., 1977, English in India: the current scene, *ELT Journal*, 31/2, 163–70.

Mehrotra, R.R., 1982, Indian English: a sociolinguistic profile, in J. Pride (ed.), *New Englishes*.

Minderhout, D.I., 1977, Language variation in Tobagonian English, *Anthropological Linguistics*, 19/4, pp. 167–79.

Moag, R.F., 1982a, The life cycle of non-native Englishes: a case study, in B.B. Kachru (ed.), *The Other Tongue: English across Cultures*.

Moag, R.F., 1982b, English as a foreign, second, native and basal language: a new taxonomy of English-using societies, in J. Pride (ed.), *New Englishes*.

Moag, R.F. and Moag, L., 1977, English in Fiji: some perspectives and the need for language planning, *Fiji English Teachers' Journal*, 13.

Naipaul, V.S. 1957, *The Mystic Masseur*, Deutsch (reprinted 1964 Harmondsworth: Penguin).

Naipaul, V.S., 1961, *A House for Mr Biswas*, London: Deutsch (reprinted 1969, Harmondsworth: Penguin).

Nelson, C., 1982, Intelligibility and non-native varieties of English, in B.B. Kachru (ed.), *The Other Tongue: English across Cultures*.

Ngugi, waT. and Mugo, M., 1976, *The Trial of Dedan Kimathi*, London: Heinemann.

Noss, R.B. (ed.), 1983, *Varieties of English in Southeast Asia*, Singapore: SEAMEO Regional Language Centre.

Ohala, M., 1977, Stress in Hindi, in L.M. Hyman (ed.), *Studies in Stress and Accent, Southern California Occasional Papers in Linguistics 4*, Department of Linguistics, University of Southern California.

Olutoye, O., 1983, Current trends in language development – the case of Nigerian languages. Paper presented at the 18th Regional Seminar, SEAMEO Regional Language Centre, Singapore.

Ong, J., 1975, *Run Tiger Run*, Kuala Lumpur: Eastern Universities Press (first published by Times Press, 1965).

Parasher, S.V., 1979, A synchronic view of English bilingualism in India, *CIEFL Bulletin*, XV/1, 65–76.

Platt, J.T., 1975, The Singapore English speech continuum, *Anthropological Linguistics*, 17/7, 363–74.

Platt, J.T., 1976, Some aspects of language planning in Malaysia, *Kivung*, 9/1, 3–17.

Platt, J.T., 1977a, The creoloid as a special type of interlanguage, *Interlanguage Studies Bulletin*, 2/3, 22–38.

Platt, J.T., 1977b, English past tense acquisition by Singaporeans – implicational scaling versus group averages of marked forms, *ITL (Review of Applied Linguistics)*, 38, 63–83.

Platt, J.T., 1977c, The sub-varieties of Singapore English, in W.J. Crewe (ed.), *The English Language in Singapore*.

Platt, J.T., 1979, Variation and implicational relationships: copula realization in Singapore English, *General Linguistics*, 19/1, 1–14.

Platt, J.T., 1982, English in Singapore, Malaysia and Hong Kong, in R.W. Bailey and M. Görlach (eds), *English as a World Language*.

Platt, J.T., 1983a, The relationship between sociolects and styles in established and new varieties of English, in R.B. Noss (ed.), *Varieties of English in Southeast Asia*.

Platt, J.T., 1983b, The implications of the Bioprogram for second language syllabus design. Paper presented at the 18th Regional Seminar, SEAMEO Regional Language Centre, Singapore.

Platt, J.T. and Ho, M.L., 1982, A case of language indigenization. Some features of colloquial Singapore English, *Journal of Multilingual and Multicultural Development*, 3/4, 267-76.

Platt, J.T. and Weber, H., 1980, *English in Singapore and Malaysia – Status: Features: Functions*, Kuala Lumpur: Oxford University Press.

Platt, J.T. and Weber, H., 1982, The position of two ESL varieties in a tridimensional model, *Language Learning and Communication*, 1/1, 73-90.

Platt, J.T. and Weber, H. and Ho, M.L., 1983a, *Text Volume of Singapore and Malaysian English*, Amsterdam: Benjamins.

Platt, J.T. and Weber, H. and Ho, M.L., 1983b, Some verbs of movement in standard British English and Singapore English, *World Language English*.

Prator, C.H., 1968, The British heresy in TESL, in J. Fishman et al. (eds), *Language Problems in Developing Nations*, New York: John Wiley.

Pride, J.B., 1979, Communicative needs in the use and learning of English, in J.C. Richards (ed.), *New Varieties of English: Issues and Approaches*.

Pride, J.B. (ed.), 1982, *New Englishes*, Rowley, Mass.: Newbury House.

Quirk, R., Greenbaum, S., Leech, G. and Svartvik, J., 1972, *A Grammar of Contemporary English*, London: Longman.

Rajaloo, D., 1976, Review of G.J. Fernandez, *Abode of Peace* in *Singapore Book World*, 7.

Ramchand, K., 1976, *An Introduction to the Study of West Indian Literature*, Sunbury-on-Thames and Kingston, Jamaica: Nelson Caribbean.

Rao, R., 1943, *Kanthapura*, London: Oxford University Press (first published 1938, Allen & Unwin).

RELC Country Workshop Report: Philippines 1981 and

RELC Country Workshop Report: Malaysia 1981, 16th Regional Seminar, SEAMEO Regional Language Centre, Singapore.

Richards, J.C. (ed.), 1979, *New Varieties of English: Issues and Approaches*, Singapore: SEAMEO Regional Language Centre.

Richards, J.C., 1982, Rhetorical and communicative styles in the new varieties of English, in J. Pride (ed.), *New Englishes*.

Richards, J.C., Platt, J.T. and Weber, H., forthcoming, *Longman Dictionary of Applied Linguistics*, London: Longman.

Richards, J.C. and Tay, M.W.J., 1977, The *la* particle in Singapore English, in W. Crewe (ed.), *The English Language in Singapore*.

Scotton, C.M. and Ury, W., 1977, Bilingual strategies: the social functions of code switching, *International Journal of the Sociology of Language*, 13, 5-20.

Selinker, L., 1972, Interlanguage, *IRAL* 10/3, 209-31.

Serpell, R., 1982, Learning to say it better: a challenge for Zambian education, in J.B. Pride (ed.), *New Englishes.*

Sethi, J., 1981, Phonological study of educated Panjabi speakers. Paper presented at 16th Regional Seminar, SEAMEO Regional Language Centre, Singapore.

Sey, K.A., 1973, *Ghanaian English*, London: Macmillan.

Shnukal, A., 1982, Some aspects of national and local language planning policy in Nigeria, in J. Bell (ed.), *Language Planning for Australian Aboriginal languages*, Alice Springs: Institute for Aboriginal Development.

Smith, A.-M., 1978, *The Papua New Guinea Dialect of English*, E.R.U. Research Report No. 25, Educational Research Unit, University of Papua New Guinea.

Smith, L.E. (ed.), 1981, *English for Cross-cultural Communication*, London: Macmillan.

Spencer, J. (ed.), 1971, *The English Language in West Africa*, London: Longman.

Spitzbardt, H., 1976, *English in India*, Saale: Max Niemeyer Verlag.

Sridhar, S.N., 1982, Non-native English literatures: context and relevance, in B.B. Kachru (ed.), *The Other Tongue: English across Cultures.*

Strevens, P., 1980, *Teaching English as an International Language*, Oxford: Pergamon Press.

Strevens, P., 1981, Forms of English: an analysis of the variables, in L.E. Smith (ed.), *English for Cross-cultural Communication.*

Strevens, P., 1982, The localized forms of English, in B.B. Kachru (ed.), *The Other Tongue: English across Cultures.*

Subrahmanian, K., 1978, My Mrs. is Indian, *Anthropological Linguistics,* 20/6, 295-6.

Tan, K.S., 1972, *Son of Singapore,* Asia: Heinemann.

Tan, N., 1978, Heat wave, in R. Yeo (ed.), *Singapore Short Stories. Volume II.*

Tay, M.W.J., 1979, The uses, users and features of English in Singapore, in J.C. Richards (ed.), *New Varieties of English: Issues and Approaches;* also in 1982 J.B. Pride (ed.), *New Englishes.*

Tay, M.W.J., 1982, The phonology of educated Singapore English, *English World-Wide,* 3/2, 135-45.

Tay, M.W.J. and Gupta, A., 1981, Towards a description of Standard Singapore English. Paper presented at 16th Regional Seminar, SEAMEO Regional Language Centre, Singapore; also in shortened form in R.B. Noss (ed.), 1983, *Varieties of English in Southeast Asia.*

Taylor, A., 1982, The position of English in Oceania. Paper presented at the 7th Congress of the Applied Linguistics Association of Australia at Perth, W.A.

Tingley, C., 1981, Deviance in the English of Ghanaian newspapers, *English World-Wide,* 2/1, 39-62.

Todd, L., 1982a, The English language in West Africa, in R.W. Bailey and M. Görlach (eds), *English as a World Language*.

Todd, L., 1982b, English in Cameroon: education in a multilingual society, in J.B. Pride (ed.), *New Englishes*.

Tongue, R.K., 1979 (2nd ed.), *The English of Singapore and Malaysia*, Singapore: Eastern Universities Press.

Trudgill, P. and Hannah, J., 1982, *International English: A Guide to Varieties of Standard English*, London: Edward Arnold.

Tutuola, A., 1952, *The Palm-wine Drinkard*, London: Faber & Faber.

Ulasi, A.L., 1973, *Many Things You No Understand*, London: Collins (Fontana) (first published in 1970, Michael Joseph).

Verma, S.K., 1982, Swadeshi English: form and function, in J.B. Pride (ed.), *New Englishes*.

Weir, A.L., 1982, Style range in New English literatures, in B.B. Kachru (ed.), *The Other Tongue: English across Cultures*.

Wells, J.C., 1982, *Accents of English. Volume 3: Beyond the British Isles*, Cambridge: Cambridge University Press (*Accents of English* Volumes 1–3 are accompanied by a cassette).

Wong, F.H.K. and Ee, T.H., 1975 (2nd edition), *Education in Malaysia*, Kuala Lumpur: Heinemann.

Wong, I.F.H. and Lim, S.C., 1982, Language transfer in the use of English in Malaysia: structure and meaning. Paper presented at 17th Regional Seminar, SEAMEO Regional Language Centre, Singapore.

Yap, A., 1976, The use of vernacular in fiction written in English in Singapore and Malaysia, *RELC Journal*, 7/1, 64–71.

Yeap, J.K., 1975, *The Patriarch* (No publisher mentioned but printed by Times Printers, Singapore).

Yeo, R. (ed.), 1978, *Singapore Short Stories. Volume II*, Singapore: Heinemann.

Young, P., 1971, The language of West African literature in English, in J. Spencer (ed.), *The English Language in West Africa*.

Zuengler, J.E., 1982, Kenyan English, in B.B. Kachru (ed.), *The Other Tongue: English across Cultures*.

Index